Wings and Other Recollections of Early Hollywood

Wings and Other Recollections of Early Hollywood

NARRATED BY RICHARD ARLEN
TO MAXINE KOOLISH AND
EDITED BY JUDY WATSON

Judy Watson

Copyright © 2015 Judy Watson
All rights reserved.

ISBN: 1507552386
ISBN 13: 9781507552384
Library of Congress Control Number: 2015900786
CreateSpace Independent Publishing Platform
North Charleston, South Carolina

*Dedicated with love to my mother, Maxine Koolish,
and to Richard Arlen*

Acknowledgments

MY THANKS TO ALL THOSE who helped, my son for the title and advice, my daughter and Mike for the photo scans, Joel Tator for his expertise, Eddie Brandt Saturday Matinee, Paramount Pictures for the courtesy of using pictures from WINGS and to Pat and the friends who knew the story, how long it lay hidden, and how it was found.

Table of Contents

Acknowledgments vii
About the Author xi
Introduction xiii
Entrance 1
"Timing Is Most Important for the Actor"—1899 3
Escape—1916 15
On The Road - 1919 19
Hitching Post on Vine Street—1920 23
Wanted: Jack of All Trades—1920 27
Fate—1920 31
Vengeance with a Capital "V" 37
"Heartbroken" 43
Introduction to the Stage—1925 47
Wings 55
Auditioning for *Wings*—1926 57
Wings—the Production 65
Wings—in the Air 69
Wings—on the Screen 73
Wings—behind the Scenes 79
Buddy and Richard 83
Addendum 1968 87
Addendum 1976 89
Aftermath 1927 93

Stardom	95
First Academy Award and Oscar	97
The Virginian—1929	103
Walter Huston	113
Gary Cooper	123
The Thirties	133
A Boat Called *Jobyna* and Harry Cohn	135
The Forties	141
The Gabor Sisters	143
The Fifties	155
The Sixties	165
Early Movies	167
History of Five Studios	169
Recollections of Early Hollywood—1975	185
Early Days of Movies	193
Epilogue	197
Filmography	205
About the Author	213

About the Author

Judy Watson was born in Chicago, Illinois, and has lived in California since 1947. She is a graduate of Arizona State University, where she majored in literature. She has two grown children and three grandchildren. She currently lives with her two dogs and three cats in Westlake Village, California. This is her first published book.

Introduction

In 1955, Horace Heidt established a ten-acre luxury retirement resort community in Sherman Oaks, California. He named it Horace Heidt Magnolia Estates Apartments. Horace had been a pianist and big-band leader on radio and television in the 1930s and 1940s.

He established the sprawling complex for musicians, actors, and writers—those people whose lives and fortunes were connected with the entertainment business. It was lovely: four swimming pools, the Aloha Room where entertainment and wonderful dinners were held, and an executive golf course where tournaments were hosted.

Mom had lived there for forty years. It was now April 2008. She had her final collapse three weeks after her ninety-fourth birthday in March.[1]

Maxine Faye Koolish was born on March 18, 1914, into a large, cultured, and wealthy Jewish family. She was considered the beauty of the family with her dark-brown hair and chestnut eyes inherited from her Spanish grandmother, an orphan, Ethel Rose Peres. Ethel was raised in Eastern Europe and married at a young age to Henry

---

1 Maxine Faye Koolish died August 18, 2008, from Alzheimer's disease.

Schwartz. Jews in that part of the world lived in constant fear of being exiled or murdered outright for their religious beliefs. America was the opportunity to live in a free and safe society. The young couple immigrated with their family to America in the late 1800s from Friedrichstadt, Courland (now part of Latvia). Henry began as a peddler, going door to door. The young couple prospered and eventually owned a large general store in Hawthorne, Illinois, a small railroad town. They had five beautiful daughters, Jennie, Emma, Lottie, Tillie, and Celia, and one son, Samuel (born in America).

Tillie was blessed with a beautiful singing voice. In the early 1900s, she met Michael Koolish, a Russian immigrant and classical violinist who had formed his own orchestra. They married and played the vaudeville circuit for a few years. As their family began to expand, they decided to move to Chicago, Illinois, to be with Grandmother's married sisters, now living there. Mike left show business and became a successful businessman. But Grandma still had great dreams of the theater for her children, Beatrice, Maxine, Alice, and Ellman.

Aunt Bea would state that all of them worked in summer stock, but Max was the best. Maxine decided to be an actress. She attended Northwestern University in Chicago and studied drama. Acting was to be the family future.[2]

The family house on Kenmore, on the north side of Chicago, was three stories tall and had eighteen rooms. Grandmother Tillie had a theater built on the third floor where she wrote, produced, and directed plays, in which her children starred.

---

[2] Ellman, the only son, graduated from Yale Drama School and was part of Elia Kazan's original *Group Theater*.

Introduction

Maxine spent her summers in Minocqua, Wisconsin, where her parents owned a cottage on forty acres with a private lake, Hill Lake. Minocqua was known as God's Country. It was a place of lakes and rivers and incredible natural beauty. The road leading up to the house was eventually named Koolish Road by the municipality, after the family. It was a fairy-tale life.

Maxine Koolish married Jerry Salk, my father, in 1934. She wrote in her biography that she had grown up surrounded by a large, warm, loving family of cousins, aunts, and uncles. Mother met Dad at age eighteen one summer in Minocqua. Ellman, her brother, introduced them. Father was working as a counselor in a summer camp nearby. He was tall and blond with blue eyes—strikingly good-looking. A cousin told me years later that she was a young girl when she attended their wedding and recalled them as the most beautiful couple she had ever seen.

Their marriage was marred by the Depression, the war, and the inescapable poverty as Dad went from job to job and apartment to apartment. Grandmother helped, but after the war, when we lived in an ancient, decaying duplex on Winthrop, Mom began to write fairy tales, and this was the beginning of her descent into despair, which suited her life better than the poverty she was forced to accept. They moved the family across the country to California with dreams of new beginnings. It did not work, and after twenty years their marriage ended. Dad moved on to a new wife and wealth. Mom would marry twice more, each marriage worse than the one before, stripping her of all her material wealth. She never recovered from her first failed marriage.

I sifted through all the family photographs, going back over a hundred years. Mom was the keeper of the family's history, the storyteller. There were bags of letters, both sent and unsent. Drawer after drawer revealed cards and letters kept from grandchildren, friends, and family. There were reels of eight-millimeter tape with no indication to tell what they were about. There was also a small suitcase of audiotapes without labels. What stories, and what secrets, did they contain?

I discovered a box of unfinished manuscripts in the small living-room closet. I sat down to read them, recalling Mom telling me something about a book about Richard Arlen. There were two unfinished manuscripts about Richard, along with a box of reel-to-reel audiotapes, love letters, pictures, and copious notes. Everything had been typed on a manual typewriter and had turned yellow with age. The notes began in the 1960s and continued until the 1970s. There were newspaper clippings of Arlen's death in 1976 and of a *Wings* memorial in 1968. I collected as much as I could find, set it aside, and continued working.

Mom met Richard at the Weddington Golf and Tennis Course in Studio City in 1963. Her third marriage had ended. This was the place where all the actors hung out in those years. It was a small but compact eighteen-hole golf course just north of Ventura Boulevard, with a putting green, a driving range, and a lovely clubhouse. Joe Kirkwood Jr., an actor, had created the golf course in 1955.[3] There was a small restaurant and a bar in the clubhouse and a fireplace to sit in front of with a drink in the California winters. In the sixties it had become a landmark for every working, and nonworking, male actor in town.

Mom excelled in golf from the age of fifteen, having learned to play at her family's private country club in Illinois. She met Richard (known as a semipro golfer), and it must have been an instant match. It was a meeting of two people with similar wealthy backgrounds

---

3 Owned by the Weddington family.

and a love of theater. She was still gorgeous at fifty with her olive skin, dark hair, and big, brown eyes. Her figure was petite and lovely. Dick was the aging matinee idol, handsome with a shock of graying hair and a well-preserved body. His eyes, which he called the "soul of the movie actor," were blue and youthful.

The pictures were in a photograph book he had bought her, and the card, neatly tucked in, read, "For you, darling, love Dick." The photos featured the two of them on the small golf course at Horace Heidt's, holding hands at a dinner party and in front of her apartment. It was a match made in heaven, except for one problem: Richard was married![4]

Ill with emphysema and unable to work in his last years, he could no longer afford to live at Horace Heidt's; even though Horace offered him a free apartment, Richard was too proud for charity. In 1968 he returned to live out his life in the guesthouse on the grounds of his own home. Where were all the friends, wealthy acquaintances, and famous people whom he had helped along the way? But that was the finale of his tale.

Down on his luck, his money gone, and drinking heavily, Richard was in a place he could no longer understand when he met Mother. Maxine rescued him from lost, drunken binges.[5] She loved him and understood the life that he once had, as she'd also had, once upon a time. They would be together from the moment they met until his death thirteen years later, in 1976.

When Dick first met Mom, he was still acting in small, unforgiving parts in B western movies, or having a few moments of joy

---
[4] She would break up with Richard many times. Aware he was very ill, she always returned.
[5] Richard would join AA with Mom's help and become sober.

on *The Lucy Show* with his dear friend, Buddy Rogers. He also participated in speaking and golf tours; ever the star, he appeared with Mom in the golf tournaments at Horace Heidt's Estates.

Years later at Mom's memorial, Horace Jr. asked me how Mom was able to rent there without the adequate credentials. I explained the story of Richard to him and mentioned the envelope I had found. On the back, Mom had written that Dick had made an agreement with Horace that "Maxine could stay as long as she wished" and "he would do free advertising for his good friend Horace Heidt." Horace Sr. was true to his word, and Mom stayed forty years. Junior looked at me and remarked, "I see. Now I understand."

Mom became Dick's muse, his lover, his companion, his secretary, the recorder of his life, and the mother to his neediness; in return, for the first time in her life, Mother felt loved by a man.

Shortly after his death,[6] in April 1976, she wrote to her beloved brother, Ellman, and said,

> As for Dick leaving me anything in his will, which you so delicately skirted in your letter, I really don't know yet.[7] Maybe he did and maybe he didn't. He always hinted to me that he did. I never asked him or cared. He was so sweet and kind that that was enough. And all I hoped and prayed for was that he would not suffer in the end and have since found out he went peacefully. He had been in and out of the hospitals so much more these past ten years and had died once and been brought back to life and had been through so much with his emphysema that I was living on my nerve ends.

---

6 Dick died March 26, 1976.
7 There was nothing left to Mom but the tapes and the manuscript.

Introduction

I took it all home: the photographs, the letters, the manuscripts, the tapes, and the diaries, and they sat in a drawer for a year after her death. When I finally read them, I was drawn completely to the stories of early Hollywood: the movies, the actors, and, of course, Richard's connection to the first movie to ever win an Academy Award: *Wings*.

So here it is, in their words and with my footnotes, and I hope that you, dear reader, will enjoy and remember another time when the world was more innocent, films were, indeed, "golden," and promise always lay ahead.

Entrance

Everyone, at some time, has thought he or she had a book to write. So many books about Hollywood and its stars have been written that my contribution, no doubt, will be just another book. The Lord knows my writings shouldn't be read by the literati, but I have been approached so often about my life in Hollywood and abroad in making pictures and doing plays on the legitimate stage, and enough material has been jotted down on the backs of envelopes and on toilet paper by journalists of every persuasion, that I feel I should tell my story in my own way.

I shall not make an excuse of my advanced years in recording my memoirs or take refuge in the fact that my theatrical contemporaries are dwindling in number; I, however, have a great desire to say something about it.

I have so often been asked, "Why did you become an actor?" I have always answered, "Never for one moment did I ever plan to become an actor."

Nobody in my family was even remotely connected with the theater. When I came to California in 1919, all I wanted to see was the Pacific Ocean, sunny skies, and orange trees. Circumstances changed my life, and by 1928 I was big box office at Paramount

Studios, for which recognition I humbly thank Mr. Adolph Zukor, Mr. Jesse Lasky, Mr. William Wellman, director, and Mr. Lucien Hubbard, producer. Their combined talents presented *Wings* to the public, the vehicle that became my springboard to stardom.

I can only ascribe my lifetime career to certain influences in my youth, which may have triggered my psyche—namely, my mother, a dour matron who loved the theater and conscripted her small son to attend Saturday matinees with her. This weekly adventure so fired my imagination that I cut up her cardboard hatboxes to construct my own theaters. I must add that these boxes were the size of dining-room tables because the millinery mode of her era ran to tremendously elaborate affairs of rhinestones, horsehair, and egret plumes. By my teen years, I was fascinated with the nickelodeons and watched the one- and two-reelers that were then being shown. I actually had a hand (no pun intended) in the new industry by virtue of hand cranking the projection machine at Mrs. Riceman's Family Theater in St. Paul, Minnesota. On alternate weeks I watched movies above Hardy's Grocery Store.

Possibly, the color, liturgy, and drama of the Roman Catholic Church where I served as the fastest altar boy on record may have influenced my later work. I was quick because I wanted to get outdoors to play football, baseball, ice hockey, or whatever game was in season. Later, my aptitudes in the sports field helped me obtain my first screen jobs. I was hired to swim, ride a horse, deep-sea dive, jump, and shoot guns in military and western movies long before I learned to act.

Now, after a half century in this business with 250 films to my credit, starring in fifteen stage plays, and speaking to audiences of thousands on lecture tours, I feel grateful for an occupation that has given me fame and fortune and the desire to tell it like it was.

"Timing Is Most Important for the Actor"—1899

No doubt my life's work was predestined. At precisely one o'clock on September 1, 1899, a special event hit 927 Hastings Avenue, St. Paul, Minnesota. I was the fifth and last child born to Mary Frances and James Van Mattimore. Two brothers and two sisters preceded me. My sister, Roe, five years my senior, had prayed for a baby brother, and upon my birth I became her sole property until her death in 1920.

My childhood in St. Paul, Hastings, and White Bear Lake, Minnesota, was one glorious adventure for a boy of my era. America was still in the horse-and-buggy age. There was the mysterious one-mile cave in Hastings to explore, the Little Vermillion River with its roaring falls that spilled over at the King Midas Flour Mill, and ever so many natural phenomena and man's creations for inquisitive children's minds to discover.

I clearly recall a time, when I was four years old, that I was awakened one night by my sister Roe. Smoke was all around us, but she managed to bundle and carry me out of our Hastings Avenue home. We all watched as the flames crept up over the walls, completely demolishing the house. It was a cold January night, and all of us were taken to the Ryan Hotel, which was then the foremost hotel in St. Paul. We stayed there for a brief time, until my father, a most progressive gentleman, decided we should go to live in White Bear Lake, about twelve miles out of St. Paul.

In those days the distance seemed far. The choice of transportation was limited to the Great Northern Pacific Railway, which took half a day, as it made so many stops en route, or horse and buggy, which took several hours.

The family chose the latter, and I sat in our landaulet between my mother and Emmy Bean, our governess; my brother Ed and sister May sat on the seat opposite. Our coachman sat up on his box over the carriage. My older brother and sister, Jim and Roe, left later with my father.

The sun shone brightly that day; an early spring thaw had set in, and the snow was slowly melting. I could hear the squish of the carriage wheels turning around and around on the wet country roads, which were little more than single lanes cut through fields. The pastoral scene was complete with painted red barns, farmers, cows, and chickens. Every now and then, my brother, my sister, or I would ask, "Are we almost there?" Emmy Bean would shush us and hand us a sandwich or a cookie to tide us over, cooing, "Be a little lamb, now." But we were impatient lion cubs, and the twelve miles seemed to take forever. Still, it was an exhilarating journey for all as we anticipated our future home.

As we entered the iron gates and approached this lovely, old twenty-six-room colonial house, so warm and inviting, with erect fir and pine trees saluting us as we arrived, we sat quietly in awed respect and tribute to the handsome mansion we were to live in for the rest of our growing years.

Fortunately, the judgment to buy the house was made by my father, as my mother was of an indecisive nature. A small, vain, pretty woman, she was spoiled by my father and pampered by her father to such an extent that she firmly believed she had ovations due her by right of birth. She demanded respect, but I, even as a child, continually opposed her. I could not bow to her queenly, imperative nature as my brothers and sisters did, and I believe my mother—more than my love for flying—fostered my decision to enlist in the Royal Air Force when I was still underage. I was well cared for and loved by Emmy Bean, a sturdy, dependable countrywoman and a comforting creature given to knitting long, woolen neck scarves. I believe Emmy had faith that the powers of her scarves could keep out all the demons of colds and la grippe brought on by the Minnesota winters.

My memories of this beautiful house and the grounds will remain with me forever. There was a dock at the water's edge, which was set up in the spring and taken down for the winter. One morning standing on our pier, I saw a side-wheeler steamboat come around the bend from the town of Lake Shore, where I knew Ramaley's Boat Yard manufactured private sailing sloops and launches. This particular launch was called the *Suzanne*, and I thought it was the most beautiful boat I had ever seen in my whole life. I firmly believe the *Suzanne* shaped my future love for boating and being near the water.

Perhaps my father had this same love for the water. He was born in Ireland but grew up on the banks of the Mississippi River with the Chippewa Indians. He spent his younger years in native dugouts and canoes on the river waters, and he told me that his only baseball mitt was one made of grass. All his playthings were either made by the Indians or created by his own ingenuity. For all the rigid economies he had to practice in his youth, when he attained affluence as a Minnesota Supreme Court judge, he gave his children all the material advantages of which he had been deprived. It wasn't too long before our dock looked like a yacht club. Every kind of motorboat, rowboat, dinghy, canoe, and sailboat was moored at the Van Mattimore pier.

However, in spite of my father's generosity and enjoyment in indulging all of us, he did believe in discipline and gave each of us chores to perform. We were not allowed to sail or use the boats until we carried out our duties. We had to earn our rewards.

The boys in my age group were always forming clubs and secret societies, which excluded all girls. By the time we had drawn up the rules and regulations, taken oaths of allegiance in blood, and decided on the password, the club was disbanded. The main objective was to allot certain members the privileges of raiding their home pantries and bringing the booty back to our hideout. For well-fed children, we had insatiable appetites.

Every family had pets, and our collection of four-legged creatures was average. The dogs and cats followed us to the tennis courts, swam and fished with us, and served as stable mascots for our riding horses.

Any male interest in girls was unjustifiable, and then when we reached puberty, the girls suddenly seemed unattainable. This applied to the same pigtailed females we had chased off the baseball field only a few years before.

My sisters and their girlfriends seemed like a strange breed that lived for hair ribbons and fashion. I knew my sisters could talk, because they were forever criticizing my brothers and me, but when my brothers' male friends came over, either coyness or sore throats made my sisters silent. Communications then consisted of lowered eyelids and giggles. For some reason I could never fathom, until I reached the pimple stage myself, this type of dialogue was good for a whole afternoon. I was the youngest in the family, however, and all I could think of on hot summer days was dunking in the lake right at our doorstep.

Our household at this time consisted of our governess, Emmy Bean, two maids, the cook, Liko the gardener, and Tom the coachman, who supervised the stables and the two stable boys, Frank and Rufus. We depended on our horses for transportation. My parents had their separate buggies, and we children had a cart pulled by a fat little mare.

Growing up at White Bear Lake was a privilege. The pear-shaped island, lush with natural growth, housed only eighteen residences grouped around the water's edge. The island was connected to the mainland by a drawbridge, and it provided a homey, woodsy setting for the magnificent summer homes—substantial in structure and artistically designed for that period.

In the center of the island was a cinder-and-sand road, wondrously soft underfoot. Carriages wound through tree-draped roads, and off to one side, a well-worn bicycle path followed the main drive. All the island homes had two entrances reached either by land or water, and both front and back entryways were uniquely inviting. We played with numerous children from the island homes. All summer long we junketed together in our boats, imagining that we were pirates and that it was our duty to attack the forts. All our families belonged to the Dellwood Yacht and Country Club, a socially active group with an exclusive membership whose main function in life seemed to be to fashion sailors for the annual boat regattas on White Bear Lake. Both ladies and gentlemen participated.

A short distance around the bay was Ramaley's Boat Yard. The boats there were exquisitely designed and built. The activities of the boatyard fascinated me. The owner had two steamboats running daily in opposite directions from Lake Shore to Wildwood and back, a distance of approximately five miles. The two boats would pass each other midway and exchange a long, whistling salute that would echo across the lake.

Wildwood Park had a roller coaster during the summer months, along with a chute-the-chute, a bandstand with real live bands, a white sand bathing beach, all types of amusement rides, and a shooting gallery that fascinated every type who could take aim. Popcorn sold for a nickel a bag, and ice-cream cones were two for a nickel and it was real, hand-cranked ice cream.

Wildwood Park was popular with everyone. Each night the lake residents would go to the park in their private launches. We would do the same things each night, but somehow they always seemed different. There was something so carefree and joyous about skimming over the moonlit waters while sitting together and singing. The crafts were not very fast, but they were sturdy with well-built, flat bottoms, and the reward at the end of the trip was the brightly lit amusement park with its calliope music (so called because the organ was named after the Muse of Eloquence). The refreshments and games guaranteed a carnival night of family fun.

Although summers in White Bear were warm and relaxing, winters were penetratingly cold and rugged. There were huge furnaces in the basement, one for each floor, to heat the twenty-six-room house, but heating was still a problem. I recall we had a fireplace for practically every room in the house on the island, and all during the cold months, we had a burning blaze in every room.

More fascinating than the numerous fireplaces, at least to me, was the main center-hall staircase. The center hall was about thirty feet wide, and from this hall ran a magnificent, fan-shaped staircase, branching out to the second- and third-floor landings. A brilliant crystal chandelier, almost six feet in circumference, hung from the third-floor ceiling to head height in the entry hall. This marvelous fixture was gaslit by Welsbach mantel burners. Each burner had a gauze mantle impregnated with thorium oxide and cerium oxide. When ignited, the gauze was reduced to ash, which became incandescent and emitted a bright, slightly greenish light. The slightest jar would extinguish the light, and so in 1908 my mother replaced them with candles that burned for as long as seventy-two hours. In keeping with progress, we later installed electricity. So very often I have looked back and envisioned that grand staircase, its exits and entrances, the landings—all resembling a stage with wings. I have a feeling that during my impressionable years, this theatrical layout had a subconscious influence on my later acting career.

Outdoors presented a primitive forest: box elders, catalpas, elms, Minnesota oaks, birch, willows, and many other kinds of trees and shrubs framing the roads. The greenery and blossoms were intoxicating in color and fragrance, especially the box elders and lilacs. Depending on the season, it seemed as though the whole island was in bloom. The dogwoods, laurels, and azaleas became one mass of splashed pastels.

High-piled snowdrifts made transportation to the mainland almost impossible—by sled or by horse. It was with great reluctance, after our second winter on the island, that my father purchased a town house on St. Anthony Hill, the choice residential site of St. Paul. It was the development of conservative and pretentious estates, from the top of the hill to the edges of the flowing Mississippi River bordering Minneapolis, the twin city to St. Paul. The Hill was a palatial community, self-contained in its growing prominence, but I was too young to appreciate this wealth. As far as I was concerned, I did not want to move away from the lake, and it took me a long time to accustom myself to the city of St. Paul.

I waited impatiently to return to the island during the winter months in St. Paul, and we moved back as soon as the snow melted. I had to transfer back to the school at White Bear Lake and bicycle back and forth, a distance of two miles each way, but then distances always seem longer in retrospect.

It wasn't long before I made new friends in Hastings. We had a regular routine, the object of which was to prove how brave we were. Each member of the group had to ride the revolving flour-mill wheel, reach the second floor, enter the Midas Flour Mill through a small window on the second floor, and avoid the tough-looking character employed by the mill owners who was waiting inside with a wooden paddle to swat us. He would follow the messy trail created by our wet feet on the floured floor, but we eluded him.

Another of our more daring exploits was to sprint over the Hastings and Dakota Railroad, known as the H & D. This entire communications system consisted of four passenger cars—two trains going east and two heading west, and both running over a single track spanning the bridge. Below the bridge was a three-hundred-foot drop to the icy river waters. The trains switched on this single track as they left the depot, and only the Lord knows why none of us were killed. We would race over the trestles, defying death below. There were also the woods, the lakes, and huge, open fields to play in; somehow our preferences ran to more dangerous pleasures. As I look back, Hastings was a playground for children, similar to that type in Mark Twain's Hannibal, Missouri. It was an ideal place to grow up.

Bertha Till's father, Peter, owned a candy store with a rear junkyard. We could always depend on Bertha for a bag of candy to share with us. Mr. Till, born in Holland, continued to wear his native clothes in America. I can still see him with his baggy trousers, peaked cap, and curved-stem Dutch pipe attached to a silver chain around his neck. Mr. Till managed to hang on to not only his old clothes but also everything he could store in his junkyard. When the war came along, he became a millionaire.

Another eccentric was General La Duque, a crusty gentleman given to outbursts of profanity. The general had served in the Civil War and come home to his rampart-styled four-story house, where he continued to keep military watch over the town. His self-designated beat was Vermillion Street, our one and only business thoroughfare, where he imposed his authority on the storekeepers, instructing them to keep their lawns neat. He was eighty years old then and somewhat frightening; however, he spoke civilly to me because my mother had been a Clark. Grandfather Clark was a wealthy banker and gentleman farmer who built the first colonial house in Cottage Grove, six miles from Hastings, where he had installed the first indoor bathtub in the town. There was a rumor going around Hastings that the Clark family was "peculiar" because they bathed every day.

My closest friend and confidant was Peter Buck, the town moron, who lived in a world of fantasy and took me right along with him. Peter was an inmate of Hastings Mental Institution. All year long he wore galoshes and a heavy vest, with a large Hamilton watch slung across his chest on a metal chain. I assumed from the billboard ads showing a train conductor wearing a Hamilton timepiece that Peter must have been a railroad man. Indeed, he told me that other than his gold mines, which were drawn on a secret map, he owned the H & D, Burlington, Chicago, St. Paul, and Milwaukee railroads. I was flattered that a man of his importance would spend so much time with a seven-year-old boy.

I was terribly impressed with the stories he told of his travels on the various railroads and the big cities he visited. One day Peter gave me a slip of paper and said, "Here's a pass on the H & D good for a lifetime." I picked up another youngster, and we boarded the train at our depot. We were riding along and enjoying the scenery until the conductor asked for our tickets.

I handed him the paper, and he asked, "What is this?"

"My pass," I told him. "Peter Buck gave it to me, and he owns this whole railroad." When the conductor kicked us off the train, Aunt Maggie came to pick us up. I was terribly hurt and felt betrayed by my old friend until my aunt explained that Peter meant well but was different.

Another time, before I knew Peter was dim-witted, he told me to save string. "It's very valuable, very valuable," he said. He had a habit of repeating himself. I collected more damn string than any kid in town, and Peter and I spent the summer rolling it into a huge ball, which we stored in the mouth of the cave in Hastings. Years later, I revisited the cave and found our mound of tired string, still sitting there. I gave it a kick, and it fell apart, moldy and rotted with age, which, I suppose, should signify some dark and hidden symbol.

Over the years, I attended practically every school in St. Paul. This was necessary because each school in succession never quite understood how my calendar of a four-day school week should coincide with their schedules. I would not say I was a problem child, but I was born with such a vivid imagination that I was told I caused more worry to my mother than all four other children combined. I admit that I was an extrovert and that I romanticized the truth and exaggerated a bit if the facts were dull. My father, one of the first graduates of the University of Minnesota law school, understood me perfectly. He must have foreseen that his legal services would be needed from time to time to get me out of trouble. However, none of my escapades were of a serious nature.

By the time I was ten, I had packed my bag no less than two hundred times, with the parting hope that they would be sorry when they found me dead. I suspected my mourners would be my family, although now I realize that a lot of the townspeople would have been relieved—none of my excursions covered more than a block away from home. I would later realize, however, that during a career that extended over five decades, there would be an extraordinary amount of travel and adventure ahead of me.

One school that I was enrolled in was a coeducational institute, the Webster Elementary Public School, housed in a gloomy, old building erected in the nineteenth century. It had been constructed from Minnesota fieldstone, and the members of its foreboding faculty seemed to have been garnered from the same mineral elements. I was greatly relieved when, the following year, I was transferred to St. Luke's, a parochial school run by Catholic sisters. There were as many non-Catholics as there were Catholics in the school, and I found a great deal of pleasure with my new companions.

Part of that era was my daily uniform. My mother made me wear black stockings, knickers, Buster Brown shoes, and a Norfolk jacket. She insisted on dancing school, and I had to carry patent-leather pumps in a bag on a string. All the children in our social set had to attend dancing school on Friday afternoons; this completely ruined my day. At the end of the first month, my mother watched me struggle on the dance floor and gave me her permission to quit. I enthusiastically returned to sports.

My father believed we should receive a rounded religious education, as well as academic, that stressed our attendance of churches other than that of our faith. He did not want his children to become bigoted in their attitude toward religion. He was a tall, powerfully built man, very distinguished in appearance, and physically and mentally alert; he was greatly respected by his legal peers and adored by his children. We boys took great pride in his attendance of our baseball, football, or hockey games. He would get as excited as any of the spectators, and we could hear him cheering us on with his strong voice that seemed to carry across the field.

At the age of eighty-six, still active in his law profession and having served as a Supreme Court Judge, he had an accident. He slipped and fell rushing to play a game of golf, unaware of some ice that had congealed on the stone clubhouse steps. Dad broke his hip and never recovered, passing away shortly thereafter.

I have gone back many times to St. Paul since then. I still get goose pimples when flying over Hastings and all the surrounding cities. A feeling of resentment stirs within me when I think that these once-small towns have since grown up. They have progressed from the one-horse-shay Disneyland image to bustling municipalities, and the beauty and vision that I carry with me of those long-gone days must remain inside of me alone.

Escape—1916

On September 2, 1916, the day following my seventeenth birthday, I left home. I ran away again, enlisted as a cadet to be a pilot in the Royal Air Forces, and trained in Toronto, Canada. I lied about my age, thus ending my youthful days in St. Paul.

America had been engaged in World War I for several years, and patriotism ran at a fever pitch to kill the kaiser.

My two brothers had enlisted the day after war was declared, and I knew then that it was just a matter of time before I would follow along. I was underage for the American services, and I could have gone into the navy, but flying appealed to me, and Canada offered a training course before the United States had set one up.

My enthusiasm for flying began when Knabenshue and Markoe (1906), two entrepreneurs in the aeronautical field, put a balloon into flight at White Bear. The men used an open meadow near our train depot as their takeoff runway, and I spent hours of my youth watching the balloons soaring over the universe. Floating in them seemed like a remarkable feat. No doubt, Markoe—my hero in sun goggles—had seen my wistful expression. Finally, one day he offered me a ride. "Come on up, sonny; you'll enjoy the blue skies." And so I flew.

That night, my father got off the train and looked up to wave to Markoe in his balloon; upon further investigation he saw me alongside Markoe. I thought he would kill the man for taking me up two hundred feet above the ground in a flimsy wicker basket, but I was thrilled with the adventure. Years later, I ran the Arlen-Probert Flying School (1941) in Van Nuys, California, where we trained flyers for World War II, and to this day I have never lost interest in flying.

The Christmas I was eighteen, I returned home with the full rank of second lieutenant. This was much to the chagrin of my mother, whose disappointment stemmed from my older brother Ed—her favorite son—having enlisted as a buck private and risen to sergeant in the Engineer Corps through the efforts of his commanding officer. He wasn't the ninety-day wonder she had expected. Ed was kept from going to the officers' training school; nevertheless, he saw a great deal of combat and was the proud possessor of a Distinguished Service Order. He really was a terrific guy, and he became a brilliant lawyer. It was a shock to my mother, however, that the apple of her eye qualified for sergeant, while the baby of the family enjoyed the rank of lieutenant. I did not receive the Victoria Cross or even the sharpshooter's "medal," which were practically rationed with food and uniform. On November 11, 1918, armistice was declared. Shortly thereafter I returned home, awaiting my discharge from the air force. My time in service was one of the most satisfying experiences of my youth. I learned so much and appreciated the patience of the corps.

I returned to school to complete my education and enrolled in St. Thomas Military Academy in Groveland Park, Minneapolis. It was a Catholic, all-male school for grades seven to twelve. This was a beautiful school covering some six hundred acres of landscaped terrain along the banks of the Mississippi River. To me, the privilege of attending this magnificent academy was most rewarding. I know I shall always be indebted for its intelligent training program. I was given credit for the time spent in service, and I might not have graduated without this credit. After all, they couldn't just flunk a veteran.

After I received my diploma from St. Thomas Military, I became a sports writer for a short time for the *St. Paul Daily News*. St. Paul seemed a little too small for me now, and I emigrated to Duluth, Minnesota, where I swam for the then-famous Duluth Boat Club aquatic team, competing against Johnny Weissmuller and Duke Kahanamoku. I recorded times of 26.6 for fifty yards and 1:04 for one hundred yards, which was pretty good for 1919.

On The Road - 1919

I GOT A JOB WITH the *Duluth News Tribune*, where I wrote both sports and amusement features. Among my various duties was to review the vaudeville offerings billed by the Keith-Orpheum (1886–1927) circuit, and any drama group that directed their talents toward Duluth. To this day, I often wonder how many newspaper and magazine critics knew as little as I did when I wrote up the current shows. I wasn't qualified to judge a good performer from a bad one. It was unfair to the public and to the actors to send out a rookie like me.

My sports editor in Duluth was Ed Barr, and my career as a reporter came to an abrupt end some five months later. I was assigned to cover the big football game between Duluth Central High and Superior, Wisconsin, played in Duluth. A heavy snowstorm had swept in, and it was bitter cold outside. I did not have a topcoat and didn't dare go out in that weather.

A group of us were sitting around my room in the YMCA. We had figured that nobody could score in a blizzard, so one of my pals in the room, a real ham, inspired me to sit down and write a whole column about how the boys had played to a 0–0 tie: their faces blue from cold, their fingers frozen, and their feet frostbitten. No running back could hold on to the icy football. Goal lines were obliterated. But the players had stood out there battling toe-to-toe and frozen nose to frozen nose.

I went to the office with the story. Barr was not there, nor was his assistant, Louis Gallop. I bylined it with my real name, Richard Van Mattimore, wrote a head on it, edited the copy, marked it with a circled B, which meant Barr had approved it, and sent it out in the tube.

The next day it was a beautiful story in the paper. The only trouble was, the game had been canceled!

On the Monday morning following the fantasy football game, I was missing from the sportswriters' staff of the *Tribune*. But soon after my climactic finish, I had an opportunity to work in the oil fields as a laborer for the Humble Oil and Refining Company of Breckinridge, Texas. After I'd spent several weeks in the Lone Ranger state, wallowing around in gumbo mud with no chance for advancement, a buddy of mine, Frank Hurd, suggested we make a change.

That particular night we were cooped up in the camp's dormitory, sitting around a potbellied stove and trying to keep warm while we listened to the wind howling outdoors. I was leafing through the well-thumbed pages of an old *Saturday Evening Post* when I read a Southern Pacific Railroad ad urging one and all to take a well-earned vacation in sunny California. I tossed the magazine to Frank with the remark, "How does this strike you?"

Early morning found us with our footlockers on the back of a truck headed for Ranger, Texas, where we caught the Kansas and Topeka Flyer, better known as the KT Flyer, for El Paso, Texas. The following day we were settled on the Southern Pacific Sunset

Limited bound for California. We arrived in Los Angeles without any plans other than to soak up some sunshine and see the Pacific Ocean and some orange groves. Soon after, Frank left for parts unknown, and I never saw him again.

Hitching Post on Vine Street—1920

Sometimes you find your way into an industry where you stand at a crossroad hitching post and wonder what is going to happen to you. Then one day it just happens.

When I arrived in Los Angeles in 1920, there was a population of approximately four hundred thousand people in the city and its bordering communities. In addition to the sale of real estate, oil, and oranges, there was a budding new creation called "motion pictures." Nobody could foresee that Vine Street would soon be synonymous with Hollywood and filmmaking, just as Wall Street is identified with New York and finance.

In the early twenties, Vine Street was a curbless dirt road, lined with beautiful pepper trees, running from the hills above Hollywood to the doors of Famous Players Lasky Studio, later to become Paramount Studios. It was all so rural. An oil well pumped away in the middle of La Cienega Boulevard and all the way to Fox Studios on Western Avenue, a distance of five miles. The streets were bordered with lemon, avocado, fig, and orange trees. Hollywood was an overgrown market basket, and anybody could, literally and figuratively, help himself to the fruit.

Vine Street ended at the Hollywood Hills before the Hollywood dam was built. I'd swear the expression "Thar's gold in them thar hills" wasn't originated by any sod-digging gold miner but by some studio cowboy as he gazed into the slopping mounds of sagebrush nestled close to the ridged mountains where pay dirt had lured him. The cowhands had come to find gold in the Hollywood studios. They had given up their thirty-dollars-a-month jobs on the plains of Texas, Kansas, and Wyoming to make their homes in the hills above Hollywood on a plateau level enough to put up a lean-to, tether their horses, and have a little space to cook. On a clear night, you could see their campfires glowing against the sky. In every other small town, Saturday night was the night to howl, and Hollywood was no different.

The wranglers would trot out a bottle or two of Hollywood gin, better known as "bathtub spirits," composed of so many parts alcohol, pregrain or occasionally wood, so many parts juniper juice, and a few drops of glycerin and water. The hooch made its way to a bottle copied from the Gordon Gin Bottling Company with a bootleg label to match. The label made it look as authentic and delectable as the real thing. It must have had potency, because they wheezed out lyrics on nasal pitch. That gin had a direct line to the bulldoggers' (cowboys') noses.

The town people liked to stroll down Hollywood Boulevard on Saturday nights, between Vine Street and Highland Avenue. Soon one would hear a sour note accompanied by twanging guitar, as the Saturday night concert would begin, becoming more mournful, pensive, and melancholy as the evening wore on.

The weekends would end with a slow sobering-up process for Monday mornings, when the boys would saddle up and ride down the trails to the studios to see if they were casting for any "extras."

Hitching Post on Vine Street—1920

Hitching posts were spaced about ten feet apart in front of the studios. This was an accommodation for the boys—all of whom owned their own horses. Riding one's mount earned an additional $2.50 a day.

Westerns were the mainstay of early motion pictures. The cowboys would hit Paramount Studios (formerly Famous Players Lasky) first, and if that studio had filled its quota, they would ride down to Warner Brothers, who made a few westerns. It was then on to Fox, who made a lot of westerns. Fox was the home of Dustin Farnum, Tom Mix, and Buck Jones, actors who made tremendous fortunes from their on-screen cowboy careers.

There were two Farnum brothers, Dustin and William. Dustin made *The Squaw Man* in 1915 for Jesse L. Lasky,[8] founder of Famous Players Lasky. The picture was made in an old, rambling barn on Vine Street. The studio just sort of grew from there. Up until that time, there were only two- and three-reelers, so this longer western feature was not only a novelty but also a successful venture. Now called Paramount, the studio went forward with pictures of the great outdoors featuring William S. Hart, Noah and Wallace Berry, J. Warren Kerrigan, Jack Holt, and various others.

For me, the charm of Hollywood is based on its western image. Nothing can ever erase the enchantment of early Vine Street. That thoroughfare shall always remain in my memory as a hitching post for all who loved the old West.

---

8 Jesse Lasky was the executive producer of *Wings* and *The Virginian*.

Wanted: Jack of All Trades—1920

I saw an ad that read, "Wanted: Jack of all trades. Joe Aller's Laboratory, 4500 Sunset Boulevard." I hopped a streetcar and sat down next to a fellow by the name of Harkrider, who sensed I was a stranger because I asked him to direct me to Hollywood. He told me about a very nice, inexpensive room for rent on New Hampshire Avenue. I went over there, rented a room from the Ferris family—very lovely people—and went on to the laboratory for my interview.

Joe Aller was a mild-mannered little man whose real name was Altschuler. His family had asked him to change his name because his brother, Simon Altschuler, was a prominent financier, and another brother was a famous concert cellist. In the early years of movie making they looked askance at his chosen profession.

I thought Joe was an old man, but he was only twenty-eight years old. Unfortunately, he was prone to blinding migraines, and on many nights we would walk the streets together to give him some relief. Some years later, he made millions heading the largest film laboratory in the world. He had invented the practice of placing numbers on the side of the film, a system, which is still in use today, of printing on a lighting level. Film can then be matched in sequence between night and day shots, whether it is dark or light. The numbers run from one to seventeen. The cameraman picks a number to keep a level to match, and negative frames are then edited accordingly. Joe kept the patent on this process, which eventually made him a wealthy man and a well known film executive. However, at that time, he was lonely, and in the years to follow, he would come over to the studio set where I was working and just sit there, not saying anything, and watch the activity until lunch break was called, and we could get together and reminisce.

When I first went to work for Joe, I was given the job of picking up and delivering the negatives and placing the film on drums for drying. I would finish each day by sweeping the small laboratory, which occupied a corner of the original D. W. Griffith Studios.

After one week, I was not only picking up and delivering film to the various studios on a Harley-Davidson motorcycle—with sidecar attached—but I was also projecting, helping develop, printing and drying, putting the film on winders, assembling, and processing; we would then put it together, cut it, and place it in cans for delivery.

I would deliver to Brunton Studios, where Mary Pickford, J. Warren Kerrigan, Lon Chaney, Betty Compson, Bessie Barriscale, and other stars of that era made independent productions. This was the beginning of independent pictures. Many of the stars refused to work for major studios, such as Paramount, Metro, or Fox. The stars that could afford to work independently would hire a company and release their own films. Although the change began on a small scale, it led to the final years of Triangle Studios, Tannhauser, and other companies that had pioneered the industry.

Film companies had been steadily moving en masse from New York to Hollywood. Universal Pictures, at that time, made rather inferior westerns, with the exception of those made by Erich Von Stroheim, whose films gave Universal status. They also gave them heavy financial losses, because Von Stroheim was a perfectionist. He insisted on spending tremendous sums of money on his productions, and he became prominent in his capacity of producer-director-actor. He also made stars for Universal, namely Mary Philbin, Norman Kerry, and Miss DuPont, who used her last name only. Von Stroheim's last great picture for Universal, *The Wedding March*, was in my opinion one of his greatest films. He made it in 1928 with Fay Wray. She was a lovely young lady. (In 1929 Dick worked with Fay at Paramount Studios in *At the Gates of Death*.)

Fate—1920

Delivering film on my Harley-Davidson motorcycle was my one entrée to the studios, and at this time in my life, I had not the slightest wish to become connected with the motion-picture industry. However, there was little to do in Los Angeles as far as money was concerned. Jobs were not plentiful in 1920. At this point fate leaned over and gave me a left-handed shove in the direction of my career. I broke my leg.

That ended my working days with Joe Aller's laboratory. One morning I came out of Brunton Studios on my round of delivering film, and my motorcycle collided with a truck at the entrance gate. While waiting for the ambulance to arrive, I was administered first aid by Doc Williams, the studio infirmary attendant, and Nan Collins, casting director, who had been a war nurse in World War I. I was rushed to Good Samaritan Hospital, where they patched me up, and in no time I was out on crutches. During my stay in the hospital, these people kept in contact with me, which I deeply appreciated. As I was a veteran from the Royal Air Force, and Nan and Doc were vets from the war, we three had something in common.

One day I thought I should make an effort to go over and personally thank these kind people. I wanted to see the information girl at the studio too, because she had cheered me up. The information girl,

Virginia Van Upp, became one of our top writers and one of our first female producers. She has passed away, but many in the industry remember her well. All of these people had an important part in my beginnings, and it was Nan Collins who suggested I try another end of the business. She cast me for bit parts in scenes where I could sit down, such as court scenes and similar parts. I was still convalescing and none too active on my feet. I earned from $7.50 to $10.00 a day, which was a lot of money for a nineteen-year-old boy, and I was kept steadily employed on bit parts. It never dawned on me to become a full-time actor.

Nan came up to me one afternoon and told me that Arthur Todd, a famous cameraman (he created the motorized camera) on our lot, needed an assistant. She offered to speak to him for me. An assistant cameraman looks after the cameras, threads the film, and gets it ready for the cameraman to use. In those days we did not have camera operators. The cameraman hand-cranked his camera. This was a skilled art because he had to crank his arm in a continual rhythm. The adage of having a "camera arm" came from this era. One had to rotate one's arm in a constant, flexible style.

I practiced this art at home looking in a mirror, and then I presented myself to Todd. He asked me, "Do you know anything about a camera?" I said, "No, just the projection machine, but I'm willing to learn."

Todd was extremely patient. He took me in hand and taught me right from the beginning to have great respect for the camera. Lenses were precious and difficult to obtain, as they were imported from Germany. There were different types of lens: the close-up lens, the medium lens, and others. They were marked at a forty, thirty, and twenty. I had to learn what distance for each lens was best. I used a forty for a figure from the waist up; or I would use a thirty. A "two shot," meaning two people in a scene, would call for a wider lens. The head cameraman directed me, and I had to insert the correct lens in the camera. We had no way of changing focus on a camera other than by using a thread and slowly wrapping it around the return of the lens, pulling the thread as we moved backward. It was around this time that the studios first began making moving shots called "dolly shots."

Before I went to work for Todd, I talked it over with Joe Aller, and he agreed I should move on. He realized I was not fascinated with the working of a film laboratory. Joe's gain was Todd's loss! However, fate would step in again and end my cameraman days.

I was probably the most garrulous, freshest camera assistant working. I was not aware of the caste system in the studios. Nobody had told me that the producer, the director, and the stars were special astral bodies visiting Earth. As far as I was concerned, they were just people, and I treated them accordingly. Evidently this was a new approach, because this industry is born of more fear and politics than any other business. It still prevails that fanny kissing is the number-one sport, and a lot of people who specialized in this made a success of their careers.

I had a low opinion of men who painted their faces and mimed. I was to learn, however, that these guys were not sissies; they could set up and trade punches with the best of them. Stuntmen were virtually unknown until the late twenties, when they were accepted as important players in the creation of action films. In the early years, the actors did all of their own jumps and falls. I saw many men die as a result of fatal stunts.

Several weeks after I became an assistant cameraman, the company was notified we were all to go on location at Fort Huachuca,

Arizona, a cavalry post. Todd's new assignment was an epic called *Quicksands* (1923), starring Allan Hale, Helene Chadwick (the former wife of Bill Wellman), Richard Dix, Wallace Beery, and other supporting players.

The only roads to Arizona were plank boards, approximately eight feet wide and three inches thick, lashed together by wire and laid over the sandy soil. This primitive, ligneous roadbed between Los Angeles, Tucson, and Phoenix made the trip extremely difficult. Trucks transported our cameras, grips, and properties; the cast and crew rode by train to Tucson and were then taken by bus over the plank route to Fort Huachuca, a distance of some sixty miles. I had never experienced this kind of travel. We lived in army barracks, and the general call for cast and crew was six o'clock in the morning, ready to shoot promptly by eight o'clock. The US government supplied all Negro cavalry troops.

After one week of shooting, the company discovered they had forgotten to cast an actor to play one of the cavalry officers. To send one from Hollywood would mean a four-day delay because of transportation problems. It was understandable that they were willing to take anybody, and that is how I was drafted to play the part of Captain Diaz. My qualification was based on my ability to ride a horse.

*Quicksand*s was a silent film with inserted titles that covered a multitude of sins that the actors failed to convey. The minute the actors opened their mouths to speak, out came the printed titles explaining the whole scene. The important object, as far as the director was concerned, was to move the players around to get in and out of the scenes as quickly as possible for continuous action, and if any continuity was lost, the story was picked up by the captions.

They found a uniform for me, and it fit after some necessary alterations. I am sure I didn't fit the part, but I did play Captain Diaz. My greatest asset, and probably my only asset, was that I had no fear of the camera. I had been around it too long, and to me it was just a mechanical instrument.

I was earning twenty-five dollars a week as an assistant on the camera, and Arthur Todd told me, "Don't take the part for less than two hundred fifty dollars a week." I haggled with the company clerk for this on-the-spot contract, and we settled for $250 a week. I still worked the camera in between my acting chores for my twenty-five dollars a week. The following month we returned to Hollywood to film the interior scenes, which had to coincide with the location shots. My brief experience with my two jobs taught me two things. The first lesson was my newfound appreciation and understanding of the tension an actor lives with in the uncertainty of putting a scene together within a few moments and then carrying the part. My second discovery was that an actor made more money. I decided to become an actor, and once you decide to be an actor, there is no going back.

Vengeance with a Capital "V"

It wasn't long after the picture was completed and I was "at liberty" that J. L. Frothingham, a producer, had a film to make in Honolulu called *Vengeance of the Deep* (1923). He knew I had been an amateur swimmer in Minnesota, and he asked me if I would be interested in taking the role of a deep-sea diver. Again, it was my fortune that the company found it difficult to get anybody to take the part with the risks involved. The diver had to wear an apparatus called the "Williamson Process," which looked like an old water heater with a glass face. The back of the diving suit, which went over my head, was an affair of tubes and cans that processed air for breathing underwater. In order to carry enough weight for me to stay under, I had to wear lead shoes and a lead belt. Diving bells were nonexistent there.

It was obvious that the industry had not hailed me as an actor, in spite of my Captain Diaz portrayal, but rather as a fresh kid with athletic abilities.

We traveled to Honolulu, and when we shipped out in the ocean to film, they put this monstrous outfit on me and sent me down fifteen feet underwater. The film featured this pearl diver who risks his life under the sea. We had to fake the close-ups; nobody could tell who was in the suit. There was a sequence where the audience would see them putting this apparatus on my head before I went down below. That was the only identification as far as my being in the picture.

When we got back to Hollywood, we went over to the old Vitagraph Studios, which had a water tank. One side of the tank was all glass, where they could place the camera and take a close-up shot. As I was still unrecognizable, they remade and enlarged the face of the can so I could show some facial expressions. To add realism, they then threw in a dozen goldfish to swim between me and the tank, while the camera ground away. They did not care if the long shots matched up with this scene; they just wanted me to register fear. It was fear all right! I kept running out of air. I choked and gasped through yards of film; the terror was graphic art at its best.

The reviews of the picture were not at all flattering, but it didn't get to me until later. One review read: "Devil fish, sea crabs, kelp, tiger sharks, all very interesting, but when the actor gets on dry land 'PE-UH'!" The picture did smell.

My qualifications for this role were both my ability to swim and my stupidity in daring to wear a thin, woolen bathing suit in a shark-infested harbor. In spite of the poor reviews, the acting bug had bitten me. I liked what I was doing. The new motion-picture art was growing, and there was a fine future for a young man willing to make the effort.

I had always kept up a steady correspondence with my family back home, and I was somewhat dismayed to learn from my father that my mother's worst fears for me had assumed reality. She felt that the whole industry lived in sin and that I was an associate of the immoral. My older brothers were studying law, my sisters were well married, and as far as mother was concerned, I was going straight to hell. Some years later, when I came home a star and the citizens of St. Paul paid homage to their hometown boy who had made good; mother had a reverse attitude. In the meantime, while I was struggling to get a toe up, I shook off her disappointment. I reasoned that feature pictures were only beginning, and I could foresee a promising road ahead.

Every completed film has a "working print," which is a duplicate of the original. I managed to finagle a print of *Vengeance of the Deep* from the producer in lieu of my last week's salary. That qualified me as the only actor in Hollywood who had seven reels of his own film, which he could show at any time. The majority of actors and actresses looking for work would carry photographs of themselves taken from the various movies they had made. These still photos helped the producers select the type of character the actor could play. And here I was with seven reels.

Few actors in the 1920s engaged agents, as we made our contacts in person. We were allowed within the studios. There was no security guard posted on the gates, and it was very simple to get inside, providing one knew the doorman. So when a picture was being cast, we would contact the director, author, or whoever was in charge of casting.

My confidence bolstered with seven reels, I took the cans of film over to Famous Players Lasky Studios on Vine Street, home of Gloria Swanson, Thomas Meighan, Wally Reid, and director Cecil B. DeMille. I had entrée to the studio, so I went over to the Ivar Street lot, which was called the "back lot," where they burned the old lumber from the used sets along with the refuse. On the Ivar lot was a laboratory and two projection rooms. It staggers me now to think that a studio that was turning out almost a picture a week had only two projection rooms. However, the studio must have thought that two was sufficient.

I had become acquainted with the projectionist when working as errand boy for Joe Aller, and I induced the fellow to show my film to various people. I had been told it was to my advantage if studio heads of departments, directors, or anyone connected with the studio officially knew I was working; in turn, they would pass the word on. Many people came out of courtesy, but they could only stand so much of the film and would walk out. I did not realize it was so bad. I thought that anything that moved was fine. I think I have seen worse pictures, but I don't remember where.

Hector Turnbull, a fine, understanding man, was general manager of the studio at that time. He had been a former drama critic of the *New York Herald Tribune* and had replaced DeMille as story head for Famous Players. One of his first scripts was *The Cheat* (1915), which created a star of Sessue Hayakawa and made Fannie Ward a celebrity. One day he sent for me.

It seemed that every time he went to look at rushes, there was *Vengeance of the Deep* grinding away without a soul watching in the projection room. He wanted to know who owned the film but suspected I was connected. He asked me, "Do you own a film called *Vengeance of the Deep*? If so, how do you happen to own it?"

I told him the story of how the producer gave me the working print in place of one week's salary. He listened, then said, "I'll tell you what I'll do, but first go get the film."

I was incredibly eager. "I have it right in the back of my car, sir," I told him.

I lugged the seven cans into the reception room, which was a shoddy wreck. All studios looked derelict, as if they were constantly going out of business. The cans were heavy, and Harvey Pugh, the fellow on the reception-gate window, said, "Wait a minute. There's a wheelbarrow around here, and I'll help you with them." He asked me where I was going, and I told him I was taking them to Mr. Turnbull. I returned to Mr. Turnbull's office and announced the film was outside in the wheelbarrow.

He said, "Fine." Then he got up, put on his hat, and told me to come with him. I didn't know what he was going to do. I thought he was going back to the projection room, because we were headed in that direction. He looked at me appraisingly and said, "I'll tell you what I'm going to do. You give me this film, and I'll give you a five-year contract starting at one hundred dollars a week, because I see something good in that film, and I think you'll make it." With that remark, instead of going to the projection room, he made a right turn to the incinerator, opened the door, threw in the seven cans, dusted off his hands, and exclaimed, "Thank God. I won't have to look at that again!" Then he went back to his office. Thus began my contract days with Famous Players Lasky, where I remained for many years and made numerous pictures.

Hope and ambition not only spurred me on; they projected me to even more spectacular endeavors. When the studio became Paramount Pictures, I costarred in the first Academy Award epic, *Wings*.

"Heartbroken"

THE DAY I SIGNED MY name to my first contract was truly one of the most exciting days of my life. I had a renewed self-confidence and hope of success in my chosen field. However, during this period of elation, I had some very dark moments. I now had a wife, Ruth Austin, to support. I wasn't of age, and I'm sorry to admit I falsified my records, but anything is legal where love is concerned. Married while underage, we were married a second time on August 28, 1920. The following year, on July 15, 1921, a daughter, Roe Marie, was born, and it was love at first sight. In spite of my new contract, the work wasn't too steady. There was an awful lot of heartache and struggle, and many days I wondered whether or not I was going to make it, despite Hector Turnbull's predictions. That is the tragic part of Hollywood; once one gets in, there is no way out.

It wasn't that I desperately wanted to become an actor, but with marriage and a baby on the way, I did not have the means to make a change. I turned to odd jobs to make ends meet, and then when I'd get a call from the studio, I would pick up my courage, and everything would seem bright and fine again.

No matter how hard I tried, this life was too insecure for the girl I married, and she asked for a divorce. It was during this period that I struck it with Paramount, but it was too late for the two of us to get back together. No one is to blame for the breakup of our marriage. The transition was just too rough for a young girl who had been gently reared and protected throughout her early years. We were divorced by 1924.

In 1925, I was given a part by Bebe Daniels, for which I was totally unprepared. The picture was *Martinique*, and Bebe costarred with Wallace Beery. I was completely miscast in the role of a young and rich French aristocrat.

Each morning for three days in a row, I had driven to location in Pacific Palisades, dressed in my eighteenth-century costume, my hair marcelled and waved, and looking and feeling more like a cheerleader than a sophisticated French Martinique boy. I felt uncomfortable in my part, and my foreign accent sounded fake, even to me. It was a silent picture; nevertheless, I rehearsed my lines.

I arrived on location during the fourth day of shooting, and I walked over to the set. There was a sudden hush. I could sense that everyone seemed terribly ill at ease upon my appearance. One of the cameramen nodded to me and mumbled something about "my double," but I didn't understand. I asked him why everyone was staring at me. He pointed to a newcomer on the set, Ricardo Cortez, and I didn't need further explanation. I had been replaced. The studio had given my part away without bothering to inform me, and when I saw Ricardo, he was already dressed in the same outfit, wearing the same wavy hairdo, and doing well the same scenes I had done so poorly the day before. Naturally, I was heartbroken.

Despondent, I got into my car and drove home. I felt it was the end of my world and the end of me. Bebe telephoned around eleven o'clock that night and said, "Richard, I want you to come right over and discuss the picture." The whole way over to her house, I mentally conversed with her. I knew I had failed. When I saw her, I thought I would say something like, "Miss Daniels, I'm sorry I failed you."

Bebe was kind. "Dick," she began, "there are certain things you have to be ready for. I was very anxious for you because the whole family likes you, and we want you to progress. But you just bit off a little bit more than you can chew at this time, so get all the experience you can, and keep pitching."

I thanked her for this advice and agreed. Then she added, "I wanted you very much for this picture, Dick, and I still think you have tremendous talent, but I didn't realize how miscast you were until I saw the rushes."

The next day I went to see Tom, the casting director, and said, "Please put me in every kind of a bit." The studio was making between eight and ten pictures at a time, and the actors could go from one set to another. I began watching both good and bad actors and discovered how terribly important both timing and characterization were. Tom gave me small parts in every kind of production. The days I spent in learning my trade paid off later.

I had gone too fast, too soon. So often, I think of the book written about the little Barrymore girl, *Too Much, Too Soon*. One has to earn what one receives, and this is true for anything in life that we cherish. More than that, one has to be ready when opportunity knocks, or risk having to go back and do it all over again.

While it's true that I did not get to keep the part, losing it taught me to study harder and become proficient in varied roles. Up to then, I had only played juvenile leads. After losing my curly-haired role, I retraced my steps and prepared for my big chance, which I knew would come along someday. And it was in this same period that I decided to try to establish myself on the legitimate stage as well.

Introduction to the Stage—1925

Mr. Cudahy had been a prominent meat packer in Maine. When he passed away, his widow, Floria, then in her midforties, came to Hollywood. She moved her two daughters, Maria Anne and Edna, both in their early twenties, and her younger son, Michael, from their huge mansion up Hollywood Boulevard to a smaller, more intimate estate at the very end where La Brea Boulevard intercepts Hollywood. The house stood on a pie-shaped slice of land, and the streetcars ran directly down the boulevard, stopping at her doorstep.

On Sundays, Floria would welcome guests, and in particular, those who worked in the industry. Everyone felt welcome at the Cudahy home. An air of tranquility pervaded this lovely family domicile, providing a haven for me, as I felt lonely at times. Floria was a kind person who understood young people.

The Cudahys had lived abroad a great deal and had been entertained by European royalty. When I met her, she lived in a fantasy world of her own—a dowager queen presiding over Hollywood royalty. At her Sunday soirees, she would wear long, flowing gowns, sit in a huge, fan-shaped chair, and receive her guests as if she were holding court.

The small community of Hollywood was groping for status levels. Nearly all the studios, with the exception of the Goldwyn (later to be MGM) and Ince Studio, were centered in Hollywood. Up to this time, there were not any trade papers, agencies, or gossip columns publicizing the news of the industry and information regarding pictures to be filmed; available parts were passed by word of mouth. Thus, Floria attracted men and women in motion-picture work. She found a niche and provided a refreshing atmosphere for members of the cinema circuit to socialize and discuss shoptalk.

I became acquainted with Rudolph Valentino (the great lover), Carter De Haven, Norman Carey (then a big star at Universal), Arthur Freed (composer, prominent director, and later the president of the Academy), and countless known figures who flocked to Floria's. Best of all, I met Arnold Grey, who lived with the Cudahys and was influential in helping me get my first stage jobs.

I heard they were casting for "supers" for a Robert B. Mantel (1854–1928) play called *Richeleiu* at the Mason Theater.[9] Through Arnold's intervention I got the job. I became a spear carrier in a Mantel production. Mantel was planning a tour throughout the United States, and I thought it would be wonderful training. I had, to date, no previous knowledge of the theater. Even though I thought it might be a waste of my time, I was willing to make the sacrifice for the sake of my art.

The stage manager issued me a crummy costume and told me my salary would be approximately two dollars a performance. All he told me to do was to follow directions, which, in my case, was to follow the guard ahead of me. The director said, "Never take your

---

9 Opened in 1903 and was known as the leading stop for dramatic stars in Los Angeles for decades. Huge and beautiful, it was demolished in 1956 for a state of California building, which has again been demolished.

eyes off him!" I nodded my assent. "Furthermore," he commanded, "when he says, 'Forward march!' you follow him out through the passageway exit." There were no rehearsals.

At the first matinee, I became entranced with Mantel and forgot I was on stage. He was such a ham in my book, the biggest, most posturing, no-talent thespian I had ever met. All of us supers were standing at attention on stage, and I couldn't get over him. From some distant source, I vaguely remember hearing the cue, "Forward! March!" Then the lead guard and all the supers left the stage—all except for me. I could see Mantel fidgeting and glancing at me sideways. Then he repeated, "Forward! March!" Finally, he came over, took my arm, and led me off the stage, and if ever an old guy had muscle, he had. He gave me a shove that I will never forget. I damn well almost went through the back of the theater.

There were two more scenes with the guards in the play, but by the time they got to the third scene, they kept me back from going with the others. That was the end of my career with Robert B. Mantel. What struck me at the time, and still does, was the austerity behind the curtain. Mantel was like a god backstage. Nobody dared to speak above a whisper. They never called me back for the next performance, but due to Arnold Grey, I continued to work in small jobs in the theater.

From then on, I began alternating and balancing my work between stage and film. The combination was both educational and necessary for my pocketbook.

Arnold knew an actress by the name of Olga Grey[10] (1896–1973), who had a principal part in an Ibsen play starring Arthur Edmund Carewe[11] (1884–1937).

---
10 American silent film actress who emigrated from Budapest and made many films.
11 Star of silent and early sound film era.

The producer of the play imported a German director, Hedwika Reichert, to take charge. Olga managed to squeeze me in for a small part. Talk about your robot of romance! Carewe did not have a hair on his head nor a tooth in his mouth; his legs were the size and shape of splinters, and he was such a little fellow they had to fit him with shoe lifts, quadruple lifts to give him height. He was further enhanced with a wig and symmetricals on his legs to give him form underneath his tights.

As there was to be a matinee performance that day, I was immediately given a costume, and it was such a brief costume that I kept looking around for the rest of it. All they gave me were little red tights and a blue velvet tunic with fleurs-de-lis embroidered all over the tunic, which didn't even reach my knees. I wore a belt around my waist, which held a sword and chain on my left side. To top off this ensemble, I had to wear a small black Dutch bob wig.

I came into the second act, where the soldiers were bombing Pisa. The stage was an interior scene of the tent on the battlefield where Carewe, a staunch warrior, was leading the siege. This particular performance was a special one honoring Mary Garden, the opera star[12] (1874–1967). As far as I remember, it was a first tryout with no previous dress rehearsals. I was kept busy doing odd jobs around the theater, trying to make my thirty dollars a week. They had me doubling as a cashier, and then they would call me for a rehearsal, and my rehearsal period was as vague as the part I was playing, which was really vague.

When act 2 began, I couldn't find the entrance to the stage tent because the flaps of the tent were not parted, and I kept getting mixed up in the folds of the curtain. I knew I had to go out there and somehow say my lines, and I did, with my wig askew and some hair

---

12 The Sarah Bernhardt of opera—famous, glamorous, and controversial.

falling in my eyes. Then, at that crucial moment, my sword fell off the chain and dragged behind me.

Carewe was standing downstage right leaning against a table. He was wounded, and fake blood, in the form of ketchup, was spurting from his forehead. In the background was the blast of cannons as the stagehands beat on kettledrums. The bombing of Pisa was in full sway. Then I came on and said, "Master, thou art wounded. Master, let me get a bandage and bind thee."

I started to look around for the bandage, forgetting it was in the chest on stage left. Carewe ad-libbed, "Go over to yon chest, and fetch me a bandage." He practically steered me over to the chest. I opened the cupboard chest and looked inside, but it was empty. Turning around, I said, "There's no bandage in it," in the finest American accent a boy from Minnesota could express. Carewe was almost apoplectic. "Go to yon tent and get a bandage from Colonel So-and-So!" he screamed. "Be gone, be gone!" He practically threw me out of the tent.

By the time I got outside, the prop man had found the bandage. He helped straighten out my wig, got my sword on the hook, which I now hung on to, and then found the hole in the curtain for me.

I reentered the tent and announced, "I've got it, master." As I started toward him, I dropped the bandage. I was only three feet from him, but I was very self-conscious about my short toga, which made me keep pulling down on my dress.

Carewe waited impatiently the whole time I was fumbling around, the ketchup a mess running down his face. He pretended to be resting while standing, sort of battle weary, with one symmetrical leg lax. He, too, wore a short outfit, even shorter than mine. As

I turned around with my hand on my sword, I goosed him, and my God, he took off! He fell right into the orchestra pit on top of the drums and horns, and I could hear him scream and gnash his dentures. The curtain rang down, and I made my escape.

The next day the reviews read, "At no time was 'Ibsen' ever presented, such as it was, as it was this time. A young actor, Richard Van Mattimore, playing the servant gave his own rendition. He goosed the leading man into the pit." Two weeks later, they reopened the play. Hedwika Reichert, thoroughly disgusted with American drama, went home to Germany. The company didn't send for me, so I didn't go back, not even to work as cashier. And it was a very long time before I had enough courage to "trod the boards" again.

Wings

~~

IN FEBRUARY OF 1926, JESSE L. Lasky, then second-in-command under Adolph Zukor, met with writer-pilot John Monk Saunders in New York City. Saunders envisioned a film based on World War I aviation, an epic of the battlefield of the clouds, and his purpose in meeting with Lasky was to persuade Paramount Pictures to finance and produce his dream. As Lasky was reluctant to gamble on an unknown quantity, Saunders spun the story plot and presented solutions to Lasky's objections on finance and logistics. The subject theme was to be an air-war story, filmed on such a grand scale and so vast in scope that it could only be presented in film form and with heroic treatment. It was to be an airman's war.[13]

---

13 All information on the history of *Wings* was taken from a brochure created by the Cross & Cockade in 1968, World War I historians, who at that time did a tribute to this film. The group disbanded in 1975; Richard Arlen was the master of ceremonies. (*Los Angeles Press Club Magazine*, November 1975).

Richard (Dick) Arlen and Jobyna Ralston fell in the love during the filming of Wings and were married in 1927.

Auditioning for *Wings*—1926[14]

THERE WERE ABOUT THREE PEOPLE in the casting office at Paramount, which at that time was Famous Players Lasky, still on Vine Street. The casting people were Edith Higgins, Fay Mohr, and Tom White. Tom was in charge of casting, and Edith and Fay handled the smaller roles. I got to know all three of them very well, and they gave me many good parts. This was partially how Paramount became interested in me, because I finally had some decent film to show them when they came looking. It was at the instigation of Edith, Ray, and Tom that I was given these opportunities. This is also how Turnbull knew about me.

Brunton Studio, in those days, was a leasing corporation, which leased space and facilities to independent stars making their own pictures. They leased stage space, standing sets, sets to be built, crews, and lighting crews. The only facilities they did not provide were the assistant director, the second assistant director, the production manager, and the cameramen; these all fell under the heading of "hiring by the star."

---

14 Dick's final narration, dated March 10, 1976.

The studio, for a certain price, provided all other facilities and the number of hours used. However, in those days, we didn't deal in hours. Everything was a flat rate. People like Mary Pickford, Warren Kerrigan, Betty Compson, Lon Chaney, Bessy Barriscale, Dorothy Phillips, and many more known as "independents" produced their pictures at the Brunton Studios, which became part of Paramount.

However, the coming of the star system broke the backs of the independent companies. It was the swan song for old companies such as Triangle, Thanhouser, Vitagraph, Essanay, Kalem, and American Motion Pictures (located in Santa Barbara). Out of these old companies there came a new group called Paramount Pictures, which had started out as Jesse L. Lasky Feature Players and then became known as Famous Players Lasky.

It was the summer of 1926. I had been working at Brunton Studios,[15] now owned by Paramount Studios. I remember it was a terribly hot summer day. I was walking toward the new Paramount Public Pictures on Sunset and Vine. A lot of new faces I couldn't recognize kept going in and out of the studio gate. Paramount had changed the name of the studio as well as its size, and none of the actors from Brunton were happy with this merger. We felt as if we had all left a shrine of historical background to merge with a large commercial studio.

The main street hadn't yet been paved, and the dust kept kicking up in a fine mist. I knew I was lucky to be on contract but not lucky enough to grab a good part, and I kept thinking that at my age of twenty-seven, I had better hustle, or I would get too old to do anything.

Perhaps it was this mood of indignation, of being displaced from the intimacy of a small studio where we all had some recognition

---

15   Brunton produced the first feature film in 1914.

with our contemporaries, of nodding hello to celebrities on the lot like Gloria Swanson, Thomas Meighan, Wallace Reed, Richard Dix, and the Farnum boys that made me feel so insignificant and alone.

Then I heard, "Hi, gob."[16]

I looked around to see who knew me. It was Charlie Barton, a prop man, and with him was Earl Cantrell, chief electrician. They had seen me check with wardrobe to make a picture with Wallace Berry and Raymond Hatton. The picture was called *We're in the Navy Now*, and I was dressed in sailor skivvies. It was a picture I didn't want to make.

The fellows were standing around, resting their eyes on the pretty girls while waiting to shoot tests for *Wings* after lunch. Barton was doing magic tricks like closing his eyes and making them disappear whenever a homely female walked by.

He called out, "Why don't you make a test, Dick?" Clever lad!

"I've asked them for one because they're testing everybody on the lot, but they won't give me one," I said.

"C'mon in," said Barton. "We'll give it to you."

"Sure, dogface, c'mon in," echoed Cantrell.

They both felt confident in their roles of electrician and prop man, because Paramount was making its first test with a new wide-angle-lens electric camera, and they were the only two employees who knew how to run it. Meanwhile, the test director had gone to lunch, and Barton, who had ambitions to become a

---

16 Translation: "Hey, man/guy."

director, and later did become a most successful one, declared, "I'll handle this."

It was a set test with a chair and table against a painted background. Barton stood by to press the button on the camera.

"Where are the props?" I asked him.

"All here," he said, sweeping his arm grandiosely over the crude furniture. "Let's go!"

They outlined the test role for the part of David Armstrong. In one scene I had to read a letter containing a premonition of my death. I had to cry, and I had to have real tears come to my eyes.

Well, I got along fine reading the letter until I came to the part where I had to cry. Nothing happened. They motioned for me to do the scene again. Still no tears, just some heaving chest movements, which wouldn't convince anyone.

"Hold everything," Barton signaled. He dashed over to the restaurant nearby and returned with an onion, which he cut in half and placed on my lap below the level of the table.

"Squeeze the onion," he directed.

I did, and the fumes were overpowering. Big tears rolled down my cheeks, and sobs burst from my throat as I cried on score. All three of us cried.

There were some other readings, and then we finished the test.
I began thinking how unfair the top brass was not to have allowed me to test, and I got more furious. So when Barton yelled,

"Cut," I made a "long nose" with thumb to nostril right into the camera's face.

Actually, I thought the film had stopped before he'd said cut, so I thanked the boys and went home.

Home at this time was a suite of rooms, which I shared with Charlie Farrell (*7th Heaven*) at the old Hollywood Athletic Club. We had the penthouse apartment for thirty-five dollars a month, a sort of clambake meeting place for most of the tenants. Before I even arrived home, the grapevine had preceded me. All the fellows let me know I didn't have a chance in hell, because half the guys at the club had been tested and dropped.

Later, Barton told me that in their hurry to finish before the test director returned from his lunch, they forgot to write in my name on the test board at the beginning. But they did write Richard Arlen on the end board.

It seems that all the tests for the part of David had been made on the same reel. So when William Wellman, the director, reviewed the film, he wanted to know who the guy was who gave such a complimentary salute. He was told it was a player under contract to Paramount named Richard Arlen.

"That's the guy I want," he said.[17]

The following day Wellman called me in and asked, "Can you act?"

"Not a lick!" I said.

---

17 The part of David Armstrong called for a young man of wealth; Richard was perfect.

"Well, I don't know if I can direct," Wellman responded, "so we ought to make a good team."

It took me a long time to realize I had landed the biggest plum of the year. Here, Wellman was staking his reputation on two unknowns, Buddy Rogers and me. Both Buddy and I were walking on air. I first began to realize it was for real when we went in to wardrobe for fittings, having boots and uniforms made to order. Then we had stills made for the picture with Clara Bow, Gary Cooper, Buddy, Henry B. Walthall, and Hedda Hopper.

Even after we got to San Antonia, Texas, on location, we still had a feeling that any day they might replace us. Nobody, least of all us, dreamed this picture would result in winning the first Academy Award.

I first met Gary Cooper when he was cast for a small part in *Wings*. It was 1926, and we were on a train going west to Kelly Field in Sonora Country, Texas, to make the picture. On the train he kept to himself, staring out of the window with that sensitive, expressive face, completely separate from the rest of the cast. In fact, he was so eloquently silent that he made an impression on all of us, and we more or less left him alone. I don't think I realized how worried he was about his "film debut," which would subsequently make him a star of enduring stature.

Somebody tagged him "Long Tack Sam" after a Chinese magician who did his whole act without saying a word. You'd say "Hello" to Coop on Monday, and you got your answer, like "Yup," on Friday.

On the first day of work, a couple of us went by to pick him up. The studio had put him in a room over a greasy-spoon restaurant with the mercury sizzling outside, and he nearly suffocated. But after he breakfasted on a bottle of beer and pretzels, he went with us to the set and stood quietly, like a sentinel on duty, observing the action.

When his time came to act, he did so with suave efficiency and an economy of gestures, almost creating a foreign technique, because these were the days of the silents with heads bobbing, arms waving, and much mugging. In the opening shots of *Wings*, after we soldier boys have left home and are in camp, they set up an interior scene in the squadron tent to establish relationships.

Coop stepped up to his marked position, dusted his shoes with his handkerchief, readied himself as if facing a firing squad, and delivered his lines.

He was only on the screen for two minutes, but his good looks and manner of handling himself caught the public's interest, and he found he was in demand. Coop and I became close friends off the set. We would work together again for the filming of *The Virginian* in 1929.

Wings—the Production[18]

THERE WERE NUMEROUS PROBLEMS OF logistics, finance, material, and military cooperation to be solved, but Lasky decided to proceed with the proposed production. Within a fortnight, approval was granted to Lasky by the secretary of war and the War Department, who agreed to furnish men, materials, and locations with certain restrictions and provisions. Lasky threw the full resources of his film company into the project, and John Monk Saunders was hired to develop an original screenplay and to function as an adviser in filming.

The War Department further suggested that due to the presence of the air service and other service arms in the immediate vicinity, the military features could be filmed at San Antonio, Texas. To make the film as authentic as possible, Paramount obtained use of the ground school at Brooks Fields and spent a year in production on Lasky's gamble.

B. P. Schulberg, then in charge of production at the Paramount Hollywood studios, assigned William A. Wellman, a brilliant young director, to guide the film. Wellman's current Paramount release, *You Never Know Women*, was a box-office triumph. An experienced flyer and World War I aviator, he had firsthand knowledge of actual aerial combat conditions, which he was able to utilize with great

---

18 This information is from a 1968 brochure prepared by Cross & Cockade for Paramount Pictures for a memorial viewing.

authenticity. His directorial sixth sense enabled him to extract all the drama, pathos, and humor from Saunder's script.

The brilliant young Lucien Hubbard was designated to function as supervisor and producer of the serial epic. Hubbard's former successes in the motion picture world were measured in financial and artistic successes. His greatest successes at the time were *The Vanishing American* and the excellent Zane Grey western series. Hubbard's excellent reputation as a capable producer was the talk of Hollywood. This reputation grew in stature each day as filming began on the aerial epic of World War I aviation. He extracted minor miracles of production in this, his most noted achievement, and he amazed the 1927 audiences with his screen magic and wizardry and brought a startling realism to the silent screens of the world.

To San Antonio came flyers and aircraft from all parts of the United States: Selfridge, Crissy, Langley, and Kelly Fields provided aircraft, pilots, mechanics, crews, ground, and administrative personnel. Balloon pilots, crew, and equipment came from Schott Field. Artillery, tanks, guns, wire, trucks, and high explosives came from Fort Sam Houston. A five-square-mile area at the army reservation at Camp Stanley was prepared at a cost of $300,000 to historically resemble the St. Mihiel battlefields. It was an engineering triumph of trench and communications systems entwined with barbed-wire entanglements.

Army pilots from the First Pursuit Group formed the nucleus of air and flying personnel. The Eighth Corps Area provided thousands of soldiers, guns, artillery, machine guns, tanks, and equipment for the concept of the St. Mihiel offensive. The Second Engineers produced many high explosives and dug many miles of trenches that historically reproduced the famed no-man's-land and battlefield. The Second Signal Company installed and operated an intricate network of telephone communications, while the Second Ordnance Company planned and executed the explosive work. The Second Division assured historical accuracy of the great attack by directing the tactical participation of the ground troops involved in the battle. No studio-process photography was used in the action scenes—either on land or in the air—it was the first major air show committed solely to film.

The result, eighteen months later, was a slender strip of negative over twelve thousand feet in length that would take two hours and twenty minutes to screen. The film bore a simple title, *Wings*, but it was not a simple picture! It was a great air spectacle dominated by the magnitude of its remarkable action and exciting aerial scenes—it became the biggest and best air-war film of the silent screen and one of the best war films of all time.

It is replete with dogfights, huge-scale bombing attacks, strafing scenes, brilliantly staged air crashes, and the inevitable "big push" on land by thousands of extras in the great, terrifying, and superlatively handled combat scenes—its excellent camera work thrilled, amazed, and overwhelmed the audiences of 1927.

Wings was previewed in San Antonio in the spring of 1927, and it was an instant hit! Opening at the Criterion Theater in New York City in August 1927, its reception by critics, airmen, service officials, and the moviegoing public was overwhelmingly enthusiastic. *Wings* set box-office records wherever it screened, and it ran for two years on Broadway despite the inroads created in the industry with the advent of sound and talking pictures.

Wellman and Hubbard found more glory in their film—glory of an artistic nature. The Academy of Motion Picture Arts and Sciences bestowed Hollywood's highest honors on the film, and it presented *Wings* with the first Academy Award Oscar as the Best Production (film) of 1927–1928. A second Oscar was given to *Wings* and to Roy Pomeroy for engineering effects.

Wings—in the Air

Harry Perry was chosen to be chief cameraman. Perry had gained a considerable reputation in Hollywood by photographing aerial sequences for such non–World War I flying films as *The Broken Wing* (1923) and *The Fighting American* (1924). To photograph the exciting action on land and in the air, Perry employed twenty-one cameras, set at different angles to catch every aspect of the thrilling pageantry. His cameras were mounted on one-hundred-foot-high towers and masked along the sidelines, and some were even buried in the ground in holes and trenches so as to catch interesting and unusual angles. Perry's cameras ground out an incredible total of six hundred thousand feet of negative!

To get the proper cloud effect so important as a backdrop for the aerial dogfights, Wellman waited almost a full month before ideal conditions presented themselves. Long shots were deemed to be more effective and spectacular when photographed against clouds so that a relation of movement and speed could be graphically portrayed. When aerial close-ups were attempted, care was taken to ensure that at least two aircraft were in the scene, crossing in direction of flight or at different, changing altitudes. In some instances the ground itself served as a backdrop.

Camera mounts were welded over the engine and behind the rear cockpits. This permitted the principal actors to be photographed apparently flying their own single-cockpit fighters. In reality, two-seaters were used, with the camera shooting over the head of the real pilot in the front seat or shooting forward over the head of the real pilot in the rear seat. The effect was electrifying! The aircraft served as a camera platform; cameras were mounted on the wings and on the landing-gear assembly. Specially designed remote-controlled, motor-operated cameras were used by Perry and his crew.

Most of the aircraft used in *Wings* were disguised non–World War I types. Thomas Morse MB3 Scouts served as Spads; Curtiss P-1's doubled as Fokkers, and a postwar Matin Bomber was disguised as a German Gotha bomber. However, a few actual Spads, Fokker D. VIIs, DeHavill, DH4s, and other World War I types were actually used in the filming and can be seen on the screen. Balloons from the Scott Field facility were presented as German *drachen* (observation balloons).

The principal flying was done by US Army pilots and cadets, but the extremely risky, daredevil stunt flying and crashes were performed by veteran civilian stunt pilots and barnstormers such as Dick Grace, Frank Tomick, Frank Clarke, and others. Richard Arlen, himself an RAF pilot in World War I, did some of his own flying, as did Buddy Rogers in some of the flying sequences.

Lucien Hubbard reported that one army pilot was killed in a crash during the filming—the sole fatality of the entire filming, so precise were the planning and execution of the stunts and crashes performed.

Wings—on the Screen

THE POWER OF *WINGS* WAS in the air! Paramount staged it grandly during its opening road-show engagements when half of the picture was screened in Magnascope, a forerunner of the popular wide screens used today. To give the audience a sense of realism and participation, backstage effects were used to simulate engine sounds, machine guns, and battle noise. Some of the battle and air scenes were photographed in color! A primitive and early form of color, the effect was startling as skies were tinted blue, and in some instances, the clouds were similarly hued; flashes of red were used to denote muzzle bursts and tongues of flame from falling burning aircraft. It was a new and exciting experience for the audiences of 1927.

Wings is a simple story of two buddies (Rogers and Arlen) who love the same girl (Jobyna Ralston), while the girl next door (Clara Bow) is secretly in love with Rogers. At first enemies, the boys become fast friends who join the air service when the country is plunged into war.

As they undergo intensive training, their bonds are cemented into inseparable companionship; their enmity is buried forever. Assigned to the Thirty-Ninth Aero Squadron, First Pursuit Group, they arrive in France to begin combat flying. Unknown to them,

Clara too has volunteered for service and is also in France as a Red Cross ambulance driver.

In an air battle, Rogers, forced down by enemy air fire, crashes and wrecks his plane in no-man's-land, but he manages a successful escape to his own lines. Rogers and Arlen are then dispatched to hunt down and destroy German observation balloons, which are obtaining vital information pertinent to Allied troop movements. Two balloons are shot down in the battle; for this engagement they are decorated and given leave in Paris, where they embark upon a series of misadventures and hijinks. The impending St. Mihiel offensive cancels all leaves, but news is slow to reach Rogers, who is a frequent visitor to the Follies and bistros of Paris.

Clara, also in Paris, learns of the leaves cancellation and sets out to locate Buddy and urge him to return to his unit. She finds him in a drunken stupor and in the arms of a Follies showgirl. Because of his intoxication, Rogers fails to recognize Clara, who succeeds in luring him away from the showgirl. Safely depositing Rogers in her hotel room, Clara is interrupted by the military police, who, jumping to conclusions, place her under arrest. In the morning Rogers believes that he has remained in the showgirl's company, and he returns to his squadron while Clara is sent home to the United States in disgrace.

The great offensive has started. Prior to takeoff in pursuit of a marauding Gotha bomber, Rogers discovers that Arlen, too, is in love with Jobyna. They quarrel, and Rogers departs with bitterness as he mistakes Arlen's explanation and intentions. The fight with the Gotha bomber includes one of the greatest air sequences ever filmed—the bombing of an entire French village. In the battle, Rogers succeeds in downing the Gotha, but at great expense. Flying as wingman, Arlen keeps the German pursuit planes away from Rogers and defends him in the Gotha attack but is shot down. Arlen's burning plane crashes into the water, but he makes his escape by swimming underwater.

Rogers, returning to the field, awaits Arlen's return. A German aircraft flies over the American aerodrome and drops a tiny parachute and a note to inform the Thirty-Ninth Aero of Arlen's supposed death. In a frenzy, Rogers becomes a one-man air force; strafing bridges, troops, and gun emplacements, he pursues and wrecks a fleeing German staff car. The offensive is at its height…there are flashes of the battle on the land and in the air as hundreds of planes dart, dive, and strafe the enemy troops in support of the attacking infantry. The wounded Arlen, with a shattered and withered arm, makes his way to a German aerodrome, where he successfully steals a Fokker and escapes. He takes off but is pursued by other German aircraft and manages to shoot down one of his pursuers. As Arlen heads for the American lines and safety, Rogers, in the distance, spots the lone German plane streaking for the American aerodrome, and he gives pursuit. The fuselage and wings are painted with the cross pattée, and Rogers makes for the enemy plane, unsuspecting that it is his dearest friend in the cockpit and not a German pilot.

Arlen recognizes his pursuer to be Rogers, and he signals him not to shoot, but Rogers shoots him down, and Arlen's Fokker crashes into a French farmhouse. Merciless and triumphant, Rogers alights from his plane and makes his way to the crashed German plane, intent on retrieving the cross pattée as a souvenir. French soldiers have lifted the dying "German" pilot from the wreckage, and they lay him tenderly on a table in the farmhouse. The dying Arlen calls Rogers's name, and it is only then that Rogers realizes that he has shot down his dearest friend. The friends are reconciled once more, and Arlen forgives Rogers. The grief-stricken Rogers, inconsolable, mourns Arlen's death.

Peace has settled over the world as the armistice is signed, and Rogers returns home. He arrives a hero, but in his heart he knows that he is responsible for the death of his friend. He calls upon Arlen's parents to beg their forgiveness. It is then that he finally realizes that it is Clara that he has loved all the while; a reconciliation and love is established between the two at the fadeout.

This, then, is *Wings*, a simple story told in a straightforward manner. What lifted the picture from the ranks of the ordinary was its magnificent camera work; the great attention paid to minute production details by Hubbard; the superlative direction of Wellman; artistic performances by Clara Bow, Buddy Rogers, and Richard Arlen; and probably foremost, the role played by the airplane in the film. The grandeur of the sky was captured on film, and so intense was this impression that it has lingered in the memories of those who first saw it forty-one years ago![19]

---

19 This was written in 1968.

Wings—behind the Scenes

Lucien Hubbard

Lucien Hubbard was born on December 15, 1889, at Ft. Thomas, Kentucky. Entering motion pictures in 1917, his first job was writing screenplays for Pathe serials in 1918–1920. In the latter year, he was appointed scenario editor at the Universal Studios. He became associate producer–production supervisor at Paramount in the early 1920s and established a reputation as one of the most capable producers of his time.

At Paramount he was given production reins on such high-budgeted films as *The Vanishing American* and scores of the Zane Grey western series. His films were box-office triumphs; his choice as producer of *Wings* was inevitable.

Displaying a versatile career, he also wrote many screenplays for Paramount, Warner Brothers, and MGM. Hubbard was the coauthor of *Smart Money*, which he wrote in collaboration with Joseph Jackson for Warner Bros-First National. This film was nominated for the Academy Award for best original screenplay of 1930–1931. Hubbard also wrote the original screenplay for *The Man Who Dared* (1939) and later became an associate executive at Warner Brothers.

His many film credits include *The Thundering Herd*, *A Stranger in Town*, *The Maltese Falcon*, *Ebb Tide*, and *Gung Ho*.

William W. Wellman

William A. Wellman was born on February 29, 1896, at Brookline, Massachusetts. In early 1917 he made his way to France and joined the Norton-Harjes Ambulance Corps. Transferring into the French Foreign Legion, he quickly made his way into French aviation and was accepted for flight training on June 29, 1917. He attended French aviation schools at Avord, Pau, and G.D.E. He was brevetted on Caudron aircraft on September 29, 1917, and was posted to the "Black Cats" of Escadrille Number 87. Upon receipt of Spad C.XIII aircraft, the unit was redesignated Spa 87.

Teaming with Tommy Hitchcock, the internationally known polo player, he wrote a blazing trail of glory in the French skies over the western front, as he was a daredevil and a reckless pilot. Wellman and Hitchcock were devils in the air—and on the ground. Wellman was credited with three victories and had a possible four more unconfirmed. Shot down in combat, he was later invalided out of French service and joined the US Air Service.

He made his film debut in 1919 as an actor in *The Knickerbocker Buckaroo* but later turned his talents to directing. With nearly one hundred films to his credit, his achievements read like a list of Hollywood's greatest films and hits. They include *Wings*; *Legion of the Condemned*; *Public Enemy*; *Central Airport*; *The President Vanishes*; *Call of the Wild*; *So Big*; *Nothing Sacred*; *A Star Is Born*, which he received an Oscar for in 1938; *Men with Wings*, which he also produced; *Beau Geste*; *The Light that Failed*; *The Ox-Bow Incident*; *Buffalo Bill*; *Magic Town*; *Gallant Journey*; *The Story of G.I. Joe*; and others.

Buddy and Richard

CHARLES "BUDDY" ROGERS

Charles Rogers was born August 13, 1904, at Olathe, Kansas. Trained in the Paramount Picture School, he scored with the public in a 1926 film, *Fascinating Youth*, that led him to the role in *Wings*. He formed his own dance band in the 1930s and went on tour, where he played at the Chicago World's Fair as well as abroad in England. He made films and recordings abroad.

During World War II, he served as a US Navy pilot; in 1945 he became vice president and treasurer of Comet Productions Inc., which he helped organize with his wife, Mary Pickford, whom he married in 1937.

With many films to his credit, he became an established star in such hits as *Abie's Irish Rose*; *Varsity*; *Young Eagles*; *Close Harmony*; *River of Romance*; *Safety in Numbers*; *Follow Through*; *Along Came Youth*; *Dance Band*; *Old Man Rhythm*; *One in a Million*; *My Best Girl*; and the Mexican Spitfire series. In 1962 he produced a TV series in the Orient, *Buddy Rogers' Adventurous Hobby*.

RICHARD ARLEN

Richard Arlen was born on September 1, 1899, in Charlottesville, Virginia.[20] Like others before him, he became attracted to aviation during World War I and journeyed to Canada, where he joined the Royal Air Force for flight training as a pilot. The war ended before Arlen could be sent to combat flying in France; he was commissioned and became a flight instructor at Toronto.

After the war he found himself in Hollywood; Paramount launched him on a film career that spanned four decades, during which he appeared in over 250 feature films, with the majority being action films. A superb athlete, he starred in a variety of roles: westerns, comedies, dramas, mysteries, musicals, and military films, during which he served in all branches of the service. He is still today[21] the rugged outdoors type that he portrayed so effectively in his countless film roles. A movie favorite throughout his entire career, he often appeared in as many as six or eight features in a single year without being typecast or stereotyped.

He made his debut in a 1925 Paramount production, *In the Name of Love*, and followed this in 1926 with varied roles in *Behind the Front*, *Enchanted Hills*, and *Padlocked*. Arlen was chosen for the second lead in *Wings* because (and by his own admittance) he was right for the role, but primarily because of his flying background in the Royal Air Force during World War I. *Wings* became an international favorite, and Richard Arlen became a household word. His many film credits (from over 250 features) included the following memorable hits: *Rolled Stockings*, *Blood Ship*, *Under the Tonto Rim*, *Ladies of the Mob*, *Beggars of Life*, *Thunderbolt*, *Dangerous Curves*, *Four Feathers*, and *The Virginian*, in which his appearance as Steve skyrocketed him into stardom. He followed this with such other films as *Light*

---

20 Dick was born in St. Paul, Minnesota.
21 This was written in 1968. Dick was sixty-nine years old.

of the Western Stars, Border Legion, Santa Fe Trail, Conquering Horde, Touchdown, Gunsmoke, The Lawyer's Secret, Caught, Island of Lost Souls, Sky Brides, Guilty as Hell, Alice in Wonderland, and many others.

The Arlen career parallels that of Hollywood; few actors have remained in the limelight and in the hearts of the movie fans as long as he.

Addendum 1968

～

The Cross & Cockade, the Society of World War I Aero Historians,[22] made arrangements for a memorial to be shown on Saturday, July 20, 1968. Their publications director and editor, on June 8, 1968, sent the following letter to Richard Arlen:

Dear Mr. Arlen:
Progress Report: *Wings*: Yesterday morning and afternoon was spent in the company of Paramount officials at the studio in making last-minute clearances on *Wings*. They seem well assured that the treatment will be given the respect that is accorded and seem to be genuinely pleased that much favorable response has been shown to the screening.

    While at Paramount, I missed out on Mr. Buddy Rogers's phone call to my home. It was his secretary, in fact, who spoke to my young son to inform me that Mr. Rogers would attend the screening if he were in town. This is delightful news, and I have just written to Mr. Rogers to thank him for his cooperation. His secretary also informed my son that Mr. Rogers would be delighted to speak of his experiences.

    The quartet is now complete, as I have made arrangements with William Wellman and Lucien Hubbard and they, too, have accepted my invitation, and have kindly consented

---

22 Their brochure for this memorial is the basis of the foregoing information.

to appear on stage with you and Mr. Rogers and to speak of the collective experiences in the filming of this picture. In fact, Mr. Wellman said that he would be delighted to...provided he could "turn you off long enough to speak for himself!" He further said that it would be no question of "what" to talk about because the four of you could talk all night until you were yanked off stage!

I cannot express my gratitude to you, Mr. Arlen, for your wonderful help in providing me with Mr. Rogers's address so that I could make contact with him and extend my invitation for his appearance. He seems to be highly receptive to the proposal and would consent to appear, and to speak, if he were still in town during the only screening on Saturday evening, 20 July. Let us hope that he *does* remain in town and that he can make it. He seems to be a pivotal character. After all, since he *did* shoot you down in the film he at least owes you something! I urge you to use your influence upon him and to prevail upon him to make the foursome complete.

If I can be of further service, or reciprocate in kind, please do not hesitate to call upon me. I am in your debt. Are you certain that your two tickets are ample? I can supply you with a few more if needed.

With deep respect,
Lonnie Raider

Addendum 1976

Mom attended the event with Dick. But in the spring of 1976, she wrote the following:

Dear Mr. Raidor:
In June of 1968, I attended a screening at El Camino College. The film was *Wings* with Richard Arlen and Buddy Rogers. Other honored guests were the late William Wellman and Lucien Hubbard.

I am now in the process of writing Mr. Arlen's biography with Mr. Arlen's assistance.

At the time of the screening, programs were given to those attending. The programs had very descriptive passages on the entire production of *Wings*. Somehow, I have misplaced my program and I am hoping I can obtain one from you or from one of the members of yours society. It would be such a great help in writing his book.

If you can mail one to me—if I remember, it was in paperback book form—I shall be most happy to pay the postage.

Thank you in advance for your help,
Sincerely,
Maxine Koolish

The following letter is dated March 26, 1976 (the date of Dick's death):

Dear Mrs. Koolish:
After a prolonged search I managed to locate one of the old souvenir programs that I had prepared for the 1968 screening of *Wings* at El Camino College. I am enclosing it with my compliments.

At the time I devised the program there was little information available on the production of the film. However, I was able to uncover quite a bit of detail that I wrote into the program. Photos were also scarce; the Academy of Motion Picture Arts and Sciences had no photos whatsoever. I have since supplied them with copies of the photos, which I used in my program and copies of the program are now in their files.[23]

I trust that this information will be of help. If I can supply more help, please do not hesitate to call upon me.

I am sorry to learn that Dick Arlen is ill. My brief association with him during the *Wings* venture was a most pleasant experience to me. He probably will not remember me, but I will never forget him!

As a curious item I am enclosing two sheets of stationery that formed the logo and letterhead of our IPS group and this might be of interest to your proposed biography. I call your attention to the logo itself and to the sketch of the pilot in the bottom of the log circle...now I direct your attention to the photo of Arlen on p. 9 of the *Wings* program.

The similarity was not accidental; it was planned that way. The logo was reversed from the photo. Each of the elements on the logo represents an element of modeling interest of our IMPMS group. The Arlen sketch is symbolic of our

---

23 They were lost by Paramount.

interest in World War I aviation movies and aircraft, and it was drawn to represent all those members of our group who build World War I aircraft models.

Good luck with your project. I will be one of the first to purchase a copy of the book when it is published. A hint to the wise: Arlen was a World War I pilot—get him to detail some of his flying experiences during 1918. This will add zest to his biography.

Lonnie Raidor
Cross & Cockade

Aftermath 1927

My next important meeting with Mr. Zukor took place after we had come back from location in San Antonio, Texas, to make *Wings*. In those days we did not have trick photography, and we felt exactly like we were at war. We were flying these airplanes day in and day out at the different locations way out from San Antonio. We'd take off from Kelley field in the morning and go out to the French or English Air Field or wherever we happened to be shooting. After nine months on location, we were a little stir-crazy. We went back to Paramount, and they were having their usual annual party, in which they took one whole stage and made it into an amphitheater with wonderful entertainment, bands and music, and champagne—even though it was Prohibition. Buddy Rogers and I had gone to Eddie Schmidt again and had beautiful dinner clothes made just for this party, and we sort of felt we were outsiders.

Bill Wellman, the director, Buddy Rogers, Gary Cooper, and I were standing there, and Mr. Zukor, who was very small in stature, was dancing with Gloria Swanson, who was one of our top stars and the highest-paid star in the industry at that time along with Tom Mix. I think it was $17,500 a week, fifty-two weeks a year. I think that's pretty good and no taxes or agents. We were watching him dance with Gloria Swanson, and I said, "If I could dance with Mr. Zukor, I'd own the studio." I didn't know that Mr. Zukor had overheard me, and a little while later, he came over and tapped me on the shoulder and said, "Dick, I think this is our dance." It was the beginning of a wonderful friendship between Mr. Zukor and me; we often laughed about it. I must say that all the years I was at Paramount and Famous Players, Mr. Zukor and Mr. Jesse Lasky, who was vice president in charge of production, Ben Shulberg, and, of course, God bless Bill Wellman for *Wings* were wonderful to me. With that association I never had to ask for a new contract. I never had any problems. The door was always open. If I thought there was something objectionable about the picture I was in or if I didn't think it was good for the public or Paramount or me, all I had to do was express my opinions, and if I was right, it was deleted from the picture. At this day Mr. Zukor is ninety-four years old,[24] and our friendship still continues.

---

24 Dick is narrating this in 1967.

Stardom

~

THAT IS HOW I MADE it to stardom. After a lifetime of more than half a decade in the film industry, with some 250 movie roles to my credit, starring in stage theatricals on Broadway, Los Angeles, London, and Australia…Of my many television appearances doing live TV in the old *Playhouse 90* and on the lecture circuit and club work, I find that my name is still more closely associated with *Wings*, which was produced in 1927, than with any other acting vehicle. To me, this is still a phenomenon. I shall be ever grateful to William Wellman for discovering me.

They say it is not difficult to accept success because we all want to achieve fulfillment. And when success comes, it is just a matter of no more money worries, of reaching in one's pocket to find the pocket is empty and being able to say with debonair confidence, "Charge it!" Not completely so.

Suddenly, you are somebody else: perhaps a sultan from storybook land, a royal personage straight out of a wishing well, a financial wizard in a blue serge suit.

When I returned to my hometown of St. Paul, Minnesota, in 1928, following the success of *Wings* and my overnight stardom, I was a theatrical dignitary destined for knighthood not only by my film fans but also by my contemporaries. This putting me on a pedestal by close friends and relatives really seemed to close in on me. I felt as if I had to live up to their image. Imagine leaving home at the age of nineteen and returning a hero with a worldwide reputation at the age of twenty-eight. *Wings* was being shown all over the world. "Well, I didn't feel I was ready for knighthood yet."

At this time of my life, being rather young and not used to hero worship, I felt I had not earned the honor to invoke such rewards from those nearest and dearest.

So, in return for their praise, I decided to put on a bang-up, razzle-dazzle, clang-horn-sirened, swan-song departure, a farewell-for-now party to record the saga of their hometown boy who had made good. I chartered a lake boat and invited practically the whole town to be my guests. Then I returned home to Hollywood.

First Academy Award and Oscar

I REMEMBER THE FIRST ACADEMY Award, because I was part of it.

One day in 1928, a call went out to gather up whatever stars, crews, and studio executives were available to have a picture taken at United Artists. It appears that a bright public-relations man had dreamed up an idea of a presentation.

In one of the small shops in Hollywood that peddled plaster trophies and souvenirs, they found an old German named Frolich who volunteered to create an original emblem signifying professional acting and production status. To further show goodwill, he bronzed the statue with a good grade of paint, and the press grabbed this hot item. The trophy was a small statuette measuring some fourteen inches high, and when Bette Davis saw it, she said, "What's the name of that damn thing?"[25]

In fact, Bette named it "Oscar" several years later after her first husband Harmon Oscar Nelson.[26] Before the trophy achieved that title, we accepted the little plaster robot image as a bit of

---
25 Designed in 1928 by Cedric Gibbons.
26 Dick states this on the tape.

studio-publicity whimsy, never realizing that soon after, Oscar would represent an awe-inspiring prize, a good-luck charm to winners—and bad news to losers.

The Oscar, as we know it today, was actually created by the Academy of Motion Picture Arts and Sciences, which was founded in 1927 by Louis B. Mayer, Irving Thalberg, Doug Fairbanks, and others to encourage the arts and sciences of the profession through an award of merit for distinctive achievement. Throughout the years the pursuit of this award system has had some interesting results. However, in the twenties, life was simpler. Today, anyone owning a television set or interested in the film industry knows about the Academy Awards presentations, which are telecast in color annually.[27] This is a most auspicious occasion, in which anyone connected with the arts and sciences of the media pays homage to those receiving honorary awards for special achievements or services to the industry. But back in 1928, we were rehearsing a scene for some movie or other when the assistance director tapped me on the shoulder and said, "Mac, there's a call for you."

I went to the phone, and someone from Paramount's publicity department asked me if I would attend a ceremony at United Artists Studios regarding the presentation of a statuette. That was all the information they gave me, other than meeting outside Douglas Fairbanks Sr.'s dressing-room bungalow.

I went over to the bungalow, and a group of people had collected alongside Doug's swimming pool—it was the only bungalow on the lot with a pool. A studio still photographer asked all of us to line up for a picture.

---

27 Today the Oscars are a global affair.

A committee composed of Thalberg, Mayer, and Doug had decided to give awards to deserving personnel for work of merit performed the preceding year. Publicity was a second consideration for the industry, which wanted to truly reward its own.

The following people were given meritorious awards. Janet Gaynor, the female star of *7th Heaven*, was presented with a fourteen-inch plaster statuette. *Wings* also received an Oscar. As there was only one trophy and two pictures to receive awards, courtesy demanded the statuette be given to the charming Miss Gaynor, who accepted for both pictures.

Others were Frank Borzage, director of *7th Heaven*; Miles Stone, a film editor; Carl Struess, a cameraman; Barney Glazier, a script writer; William Cameron Menzie, an art designer; and several other gentlemen whose names escape me.

Then the photographer lined up the remaining people such as William Wellman, director of *Wings*; Lucien Hubbard, the producer; Doug Sr.; Buddy Rogers; and me. I have a copy of that still picture.[28] I recall I wore white pants and stood right next to Doug with my hand in my pants pocket, just like him. Doug took one look at the plaster-of-paris statue and said we could throw it over on Stage 2, and I dared him to.

I was asked to appear as a representative of *Wings*, which, jointly with *7th Heaven*, received recognition from the newly formed Motion Pictures Arts and Sciences Foundation.

The Trades stressed that *Wings* had received the first Academy Award for best production and photography, *7th Heaven* for acting and story.

---

28 Now in the Martha Herrick Library.

After the picture was taken, we adjourned to a little restaurant for lunch. And that is the story of the first Academy Awards.[29]

I am so glad to have been a part of it

---

29 This narration is dated March 10, 1976. Richard Arlen died on March 26, 1976.

ALL TALKING ACTION SPECIAL

•

Gary Cooper, new male idol of American fans, Walter Huston, stage star, Richard Arlen, Mary Brian and a big cast, in a swift-moving love-drama from Owen Wister's well known novel. With all the far-flung panorama of the gorgeous West as a background. Directed by Victor Fleming, who made "Abie's Irish Rose."

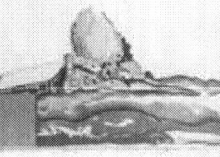

THE VIRGINIAN

GARY COOPER, WALTER HUSTON, RICHARD ARLEN *and* MARY BRIAN

The Virginian—1929

Therefore Trampas spoke: "Your bet you son of a..."
The Virginian's pistol came out, and his land lay on the table, holding it unaimed.
And with a voice as gentle as ever, the voice that sounded almost like a caress, but drawling little more than usual, so that there was almost a space between each word, he issued his orders to the man.
"Trampas, if you wanna call me that, smile," and looked at Trampas across the table.
Yes, the voice was gentle. But in my ears it seemed as if somewhere the bell of death was ringing; in silence...[30]

THE MOVIE *THE VIRGINIAN* WAS based on a fictionalized true story of the old west by Owen Wister, a novelist (1902). It would become a classic. It was a love story, but the main theme based on history was a dispute between the large cattle ranchers and theft on the range from lesser cowboys. Frontier justice in those days required lynching. The Virginian, a restless drifter, known only by this name and never his actual name, became the leader of the western frontier, by his quiet presence. I played the part of his best friend, Steve, and came under the evil influence of Huston, who played the part of Trampas, a rustler. Once caught, death by hanging was the only answer for quick justice in the wilderness of the west. Coop, as the

---
30 Quote from *The Virginian* by Owen Wister.

Virginian, had to watch while I was hung. He was torn apart as he realized what our friendship had meant and discovered that justice is never simple. Molly, his bride-to-be, was horrified by what she had seen. Their pending marriage was threatened by Trampas. This was the first classic "showdown," I believe, in fiction. Trampas shot first and missed, and shooting in self-defense, the Virginian killed him. The lone cowboy rode on and into film history.

In April of 1929, Paramount decided to try an experiment and do an outdoor film in sound. It starred Mary Brian, Walter Huston, Eugene Pallette, Coop, and me.[31] The movie would be shot in black and white using natural lighting. To compensate the actors wore very heavy makeup, including lipstick and mascara, as had been used in the silent movies.

Up to this time, the studios had thought it was impossible to make an outdoor talkie with all the complications of interfering sounds of birds and animals, the rustle of leaves, overcast clouds, the cattle, and anything else. It was the first time a talking movie was made on location, and it rose above the average type of cowboy picture because of Wister's wonderful writing. Jesse Lasky predicted correctly that this movie would set a standard for all future adult cowboy movies.

We found ourselves up in the High Sierras of Sonora, California, with tons of audio equipment, which we hauled up the mountain by cable pulled by both horse and man to film this, the very first outdoor talking movie. I had made several sound pictures prior to this and was considered a veteran. I looked forward to the part of Steve, a good character part. Coop was cast as the Virginian, an excellent role, and having no sound experience, he was scared to death. Victor Fleming [32] was our director.

---

31 This movie would make a star out of Gary Cooper.
32 Fleming won an Oscar for best direction for *Gone with the Wind* in 1939.

Early each morning we would saddle up, slap the horses' sides, and say, "Come on, Shamrock; let it all out now." Then with grunts and heaves they'd comply with Mother Nature. One morning we got an earlier-than-usual sunrise call to move up the trail, and there wasn't any time to employ these tactics. Coop and I started walking our horses on this steep incline where I said my line, "This way," and we continued going uphill. Our soundman, Earl Hayman, down below in a ravine with his equipment, was hidden from view. Hayman was a city man, a dignified citizen who refrained from obscene language. The gassy horses, however, were unaware they were on camera, and they plodded on, snorting and raising their tails. Coop had just rolled a cigarette and was taking a puff when Hayman unexpectedly jumped out of the brush, perspiration freckling his face, his earphones dangling from his head, shouting, "My God, stop! Something's gone wrong! I hear explosions!"

Coop, sitting unperturbed on his horse, turned to the engineer and said in his unruffled voice, "Shucks, man, ain't you ever heard a horse fart?"

With all his cool, Coop was in such awe of the sound camera that he almost quit when he had to do a love scene with Mary Brian. Our director, Victor Fleming, had no patience with the big cowboy, because some months earlier, while making a silent film, Coop had romanced Lupe Velez, who up to then had been the director's girl. Fleming displayed his hostility, and whenever Coop fluffed a line, which was often, Fleming would rasp for retakes, which unnerved the actor. For two days Coop and Mary sat on a rock for a scene and only managed three lines of dialogue. I took Coop aside and made a deal wherein I would climb into a tree overhead and give him his cues, when to say, "Yup" and "Nope." These were about all his lines consisted of until his big speech when Mary came to her line, which was, "Why didn't you like that book?" referring to Romeo and Juliet.

Coop's reply was, "I don't think a fellow who runs up and down rope ladders has much courage."

Mary answered, "Well, what would you do?"

And that's where he always blew his next line, which was, "I would just walk up to the door and knock and tell her old man that I want to marry her." It was just too much for the tall man to remember.

From my treetop position, I could see Fleming on the ground. The poor guy would scratch his head in bewilderment as Coop spoke his lines in measured rote, raising his eyes, but keeping his head fixed on target. I thought we were getting along fine in spite of retakes. We were just finishing the last few words when Fleming spied me lying spread-eagled on a tree branch. Enraged, he tore his cap off his head and roared, "*Cut!*" with such venom, I lost my balance. The camera caught me falling downward saying Coop's lines.

Coop, for all his seeming nonchalance, felt insecure in his work and subconsciously began to develop facial mannerisms, which later endeared him to his audiences. He would rub or pull on his nose, twitch his mouth, tug on his ear, or screw up his face—all necessary devices to give him time to think of his next lines. As he improved his acting, he gained confidence, but the small idiosyncrasies remained. Just watch any old television movie he's in, and you'll see Coop massaging his features, struggling for his lines. He had developed a speech habit of drawling to cover his crooked front teeth, which came off in the sound track as if he were deliberately throwing away lines. I desperately wanted to help him overcome his fears, and fortunately, help came in the form of Walter Huston, who became Coop's coach and mentor.

The Virginian—1929

When talkies came in, many able actors saw their careers finished before they perfected the canned sound, so the studios began importing stage actors. Screen fright, fear of the microphone, and new acting methods, wherein words substituted for pantomime, created havoc among professional screen actors. It was imperative to act while speaking, because there were no more titles to insert to explain what was going on after one finished the scene. One had to underplay facial expressions, and the quality of one's voice became all-important. If a man's voice was weak, without resonance, or high in pitch, the actor had no chance. Too often, fear of the microphone would send his voice up an octave. He might begin speaking in a deep bass, but fright would send it up to the stars and send the audience into hysterics.

Characteristic of the times, Paramount contracted Walter Huston to play Trampas, the classic villain in *The Virginian*, and when Coop heard that the legitimate stage actor was going to join our company, he complained, "I'm sick and tired of those guys coming here."

I knew he was apprehensive of being cast with a great pro, so I queried, "How do you know he won't turn out to be one of the nicest people we have ever had the good fortune to meet? He may help you in your work. The better the actors around you, the better you're going to look." Coop didn't place much faith in that idea, and I began having my own misgivings, thinking his gripes might be justifiable. If the contrast were to our disadvantage, we would look like two-bit cowpokes. Fortunately, the unexpected happened.

One morning the cast was standing on the set waiting for the crew to get ready. It was early, and the sun was high, promising another blistering-hot workday. Presently, Huston joined the group, and something in his hangdog stance impressed Coop and me, for Huston looked like a whipped cur.

I nudged Coop. "What's bothering him?"

"Durned if I know. You'd think a city fellow would have more whup."

"Think he's sick?"

"Nope. Think he's grieving over that costume he's wearing. Downright silly looking."

"He does look like a drugstore cowboy," I agreed.

Actually, Huston's costume had the unsavory appearance of a ten, twenty, and thirty western melodrama. His gauntlets were old-fashioned, his hat had the broad brim of a Mexican conquistador's sombrero, his outsize spurs were ridiculous, and his rawhide chaps looked as if he intended to settle down permanently in the dense chaparrals.

In his inimitable walk, Coop sauntered over to Huston and asked, "Mr. Huston, you mind answering a personal question? Did you get your clothes from wardrobe or from the Salvation Army?"

Huston grinned. "This is the mad dream of the wardrobe man, fellows."

"Yup." Coop shook his head. "Too bad you couldn't get outfitted in Hollywood instead of the Wild West."

Huston's problem costume had erupted from bad timing, as he was brought in from New York to San Francisco and then traveled by rain to Modesto, where he was picked up by car. This was his second film after a long and successful stage career. He had been delayed in New York and did not arrive on location with the company from Hollywood. The director had shot all around his scenes until he joined us, but by this time the wardrobe department had to dress him in whatever meager offering they had left. We felt terribly embarrassed for the man, because he was almost twice our age and twice the actor.

What surprised me next was Coop's insight of understanding Huston's predicament. The lone cowboy didn't seem to care about clothes, nor did he own more than one suit.

"Come on," Coop signaled, "Dick has a car, and we've got time before they start shooting."

Neither Huston nor I understood what he was saying until I remembered we were in Sonora, which boasted a general store where we had driven to town the day before for some Bull Durham tobacco for Coop. The three of us got in my car and drove fast over dirty roads and chuckholes as deep and sharp as rock gorges. On the drive Huston felt it necessary to explain, "I really feel miserable in this outfit." His expressive hands gestured the indignity of his plight.

We made it back to the set on time. Fleming even liked the way Trampas looked—more like the book engravings. Huston walked toward the camera in the rugged work clothes of a man of the plains who rode the saddle from sunup to sundown. He resembled the villain character he played now that he was no longer garbed in the effete costume he'd been issued.

Huston appreciated Coop's thoughtfulness, and in return he helped him with his acting problems. What had begun as an unpredicted guess at a probable friendly relationship with the famous stage star progressed into a solid kinship among the three of us.

I believe this incident was pivotal in triggering interest in Coop's own appearance. As far as I knew, he had never taken a second look at what he was wearing, other than boots and Levis. He didn't seem to care about custom-tailored suits or fashion in general, nor can I remember his wearing a tie.

Thirteen or fourteen weeks later, we returned to Hollywood and finished the picture.

Walter and I had become close friends while filming *The Virginian*. When the company completed work on location at Sonora, California, we had to return to Hollywood to do the final scenes. All of us—cast and crew—were in our hotel rooms this Sunday night packing our bags for our return trips. It was late evening, I had an empty car to drive back home, and I suggested, "Walter, tomorrow we have to work at Paramount Ranch, and you're going to be too tired to start looking for a hotel room in Los Angeles, so stay with me until you're settled." My guesthouse was available. He accepted and remained as my guest for a whole year, a wonderful year that gave us time to really get to know each other.

Walter Huston

Memories...when I was a little boy in St. Paul, Minnesota, my family owned the property where the Orpheum Theatre was built. I was a regular matinee attendant, and one of the comedy acts that played the Orpheum circuit was a two-man team called Whipple & Huston, in which Huston portrayed a paperhanger. All the way through the review, Huston kept up a patter and sang little jingles—one of which went, "I haven't got the do re mi"—while he papered the wrong walls and papered people's heads. It really was a funny act.

Years later after Walter Huston had become famous on the New York stage, he made a film with Claudette Colbert called *The Hole in the Wall* (1929), which led to his being cast as Trampas in *The Virginian*. Then he made two pictures for Paramount, playing opposite Kay Francis and Ruth Chatterton. Ironically, in spite of the large sums of money he'd earned, he was still singing, "I haven't got the do re mi," only this time it wasn't any act. He was making stiff alimony payments to his ex-wife, and he desperately wanted to give her a final lump settlement.

After a year had passed, Walter took an apartment and agreed to make some low-budget pictures for Warner Brothers, who offered him $25,000 a picture, a fabulous sum for that time. He knew he was making inferior films, which were damaging to his image, but Walter was determined to pay off his wife. After two years of working at Warner Brothers, there came a lull with nothing scheduled ahead for him, so he went to MGM and accepted a long-term contract with a starting salary of $1,500 a week. This was a big dip for Walter, not only in salary but also in the unsatisfactory roles and inferior films they gave him. He continued under contract to make pictures that were bad for him. He endured this subjugation in quiet humility, fully realizing how much he was hurting his acting record and destroying himself.

One morning my phone rang. It was Walter. He wanted to see me, and I could tell from the jubilant tones in his voice that he had good news. I asked him to come by, and when he arrived I saw a vibrant, independent individual emerge from this man whose personality had been throttled for years. We walked out on my patio for coffee, and he could hardly contain himself.

"Dick," he told me, "I'm off the hook. My debt is paid up, and now I'm through."

I thought he was referring to his divorce settlement, and he had my sympathy because I'd had my share of huge alimony payments, but he meant more.

"What do you mean, you're through?" I asked.

"I mean I just quit Metro-Goldwyn-Mayer for good!" he said.

"What happened?" I asked.

"I was playing a lousy little part in a Max Baer picture," he continued, "where I was his manager. What finally finished me was when I had to give Max instructions in a scene, which called for his slapping my face and spitting on it! It killed me. It was my last scene in the picture and my last picture for Metro-Goldwyn-Mayer or any other motion-picture company. Someday, maybe, I'll do another picture, but only on my terms." He spoke softly with the dignity of a human who had endured much suffering. This was the fourth time Walter had made a pitch at a career.

On this peaceful morning when we sat beneath the trees and he told me he was through with pictures, I felt great distress for him. He must have then been close to fifty-three years old. I was thirty-four, and I thought he was an old man and finished.

"What are you going to do now?" I asked him.

"I'm going back to the stage."

That made sense to me. He had made an outstanding name for himself with *Elmer the Great, Desire under the Elms,* and *Mr. Pitt.* I wondered if he was going to resurrect one of those classics. Then, he surprised me with his next statement.

"I've got a new play called *Dodsworth.* Will you read it and let me know what you think of it?"

I read the play, and when he asked my opinion, I told him I thought it was very interesting. "But that's not enough," I said. "I'll have to read it again and know what to look for. I'm not sure about the relationship of the people."

Walter explained the relationship of the characters, and when I read it again, it was very clear. Then he asked me if I liked it any better, and I did. We discussed different points of the play, and then he asked, "Do you think it will do?"

"Walter," I said, "it seems right for you, but how are you going to produce it?"

And he answered, "With very little money."

This bright fellow was a sort of jack-of-all-trades. He was a good carpenter, painter, and designer, as well as an actor. He put all his skills together and built a stage with motorized revolving doors and scenery. It was novel and practical. There were only a few mechanized stages in use in New York at that time.

Dodsworth opened in March 1934 in New York City and was never "tried out" away from that city.

Just before the play opened, I was in New York getting ready to sail on the *Majestic* to England. I called Walter, and he told me to come over to watch a dress rehearsal. I sat through three acts absolutely spellbound.

When the play was over, he asked, "What did you think of it, Dick?"

"Walter, it was magnificent! Believe me, if I can sit in this theater, with only a few people in the audience, and not want the play to end, then you have put a spell on me. It was hard for me to believe you were Walter Huston and not Sam Dodsworth."

Before I sailed the following day, I asked him to let me know about the reviews. This was the early period of ship-to-shore telephone communications. I didn't expect a telephone call until after the critics had given an accounting of the show. I was called from the ship salon earlier than I had anticipated. It was Walter, and there was so much static and interference on the line that we could hardly hear each other. It sounded like, "It's a smash hit." At least I thought he'd said that.

I immediately sent a radiogram explaining the connection was poor. I wrote: "Was it a smash hit as you said?"

I received a radiogram in return saying: "It was bigger than that. Sold out three months in advance within twenty-four hours."

Six months later I returned to America and went to the theater to see the play again. It was better than before. Many times during a play, the actors can improvise and keep building incidents that happen, which improve the play. A new idea comes along, the actor springs it, and a good cast picks it right up without the audience knowing what is happening in front of them. So when I saw *Dodsworth* a second time, I never thought I was in a theater—I thought I was a part of it. Now, many years later, that exciting evening is still vividly etched on my mind. Much of the credit for the success of *Dodsworth* belonged to his producer, Arthur Hopkins,[33] a most astute gentlemen.

After a year's run of the show in New York, Walter decided to take the play on tour. The theaters were too small to handle his portable stages. It was found necessary to lease auditoriums. I remember I was playing in a golf tournament in Sacramento, California. Walter Hagen[34] was my partner, and we drew remarkable galleries. Walter Huston was also playing Sacramento and drawing tremendous capacity audiences. I met him after his show one evening, and he told me the show was playing to sold-out houses of five thousand people per performance, six evening and two matinee performances weekly. His take averaged eight dollars a seat, or some $40,000 a performance, and he owned the controlling interest in the play.

---

33 Hopkins produced and directed eighty plays on Broadway.
34 One of the great golfers of the twentieth century.

Following his tour, Walter came back to Hollywood and made a deal with producer Sam Goldwyn, who had a fair amount of hits to his record, to film *Dodsworth*.

About that time, Mary Astor[35] was in a bind. She had written an exceptionally personal diary. Her husband, Dr. Thorpe, had confiscated it, made public display of her indiscretions, and tried to ruin her career. Her close friends were unconcerned as to the qualifications of her infidelities and had only contempt for the doctor.

I had a little homecoming party at my Toluca Lake home for Walter and invited Mary along with other guests. Walter took her aside and asked, "Mary, what are you doing with yourself these days?"

"Walter," she admitted, "since I've written my diary, I haven't done much of anything."

"Oh, that." He brushed off her apologies. "You know something, you'd make a wonderful 'Fran' in *Dodsworth*. Have you seen it?" She nodded. "Would you like to play it?"

She replied, "Yes, I've seen it, and I would love to."

"Fine. I'll talk to Sam in the morning."

The following day he went to Mr. Goldwyn, and thanks to Walter, Mary Astor had a whole new career in front of her. His progress never stopped from then on, because he never allowed himself to get backed into a corner again. He not only selected his own parts but also chose the players surrounding him.

---

35 Academy Award–winning actress of the silent and talking movies (1906–1987).

I felt very honored, therefore, when he asked me to play a part in *Duel in the Sun*, a film produced by David Selznik, starring Jennifer Jones, Gregory Peck, Joseph Cotton, Charles Bickford, and Walter (1946). I was honored, but unfortunately, I had to turn it down as I had other film commitments. Charles Bickford did the role he had selected for me and did it very well. In the film, Walter played a fire-and-brimstone minister, and he was electrifying. He was only on the screen for seven minutes, but when you left the theater, you remembered this factious orator, this demagogue who weaved his spell. His transformations were sublime. Walter knew he could take a small part and create more with it than a lead part. A good businessman—he received $150,000 for his characterization. I call that good acting!

I recall that in 1945 Walter wanted me to do a play with him in New York. I had just closed in a show called *Too Hot for Maneuvers* in New York City, and the play had had an excellent run. If the times had been different, and I had not been under contract to make some films on the West Coast, I might have considered it. However, at that time I was disenchanted with the legitimate theater during the war and with the individual deportment of people connected with the theater. In fact, I was disillusioned with Broadway, and I wanted to go home to California. I sincerely regretted missing out on this opportunity of working with him.

September Song (1944) was Walter's last stage appearance. He was very much in demand, and he could easily have retired at this time with wealth and acclaim. In *September Song*, he sang his lament, a theme song describing the discrepancy between the heroine's and his ages, with the same lack of voice he'd had with his *Whipple & Houston* almost three decades back. He still had that magic to make his audiences cry.

One of his last films was the *Furies* with Barbara Stanwyck (1950). He was sixty-three at the time, and he played the part of an older lover, a June-and-January romance, perpetuating his magnificent appeal, endearing himself to his fans for time eternal.

Gary Cooper

In Cinemaland first names identify the individual, such as Judy, Cary, Zsa Zsa, Mickey, Liz, Greer, or Jimmy. The name Gary blends with Cooper, a shy, inarticulate young actor whom I met during my early working years for Paramount Studios. "Coop," as we called him, became my lifelong friend until he died.

Gary Cooper was six feet four, a lean fellow, a chronic tiptoer from wearing high-heeled boots, and a master of the soft-spoken word. He had a physical repose that was not an affectation and exhibited a saturnine expression, which belied his fondness for humor. He had a separate communion with himself. Coop was a big chuckler. He was always chuckling inside, and when his sense of the ridiculous reached a peak, he would bust out all over.

The transformation from soldier of fortune to "the glass of fashion and the mould of form" (*Hamlet*) was affected by outside influences. As Coop became more popular on the screen, the magazines, trade papers, and dailies gave him more space. He didn't court publicity, much preferring to remain inconspicuous, both on the studio lot and in his personal life. However, romance in glitter town jolted him to front page prominence. He had started to date Lupe Velez,[36] a vivacious Mexican actress labeled "the Mexican Spitfire" whom he met in 1929 when they starred together in *The Wolf Song*.

Lupe was a big star in her country, as well as the United States, but after she took one look at the big cowboy, she threw away her mantilla. It was a repeat of the old saw of opposites attracting, with stiletto improvisations, because Coop was as slow and deep as a country well, and Lupe as vacillating as quicksilver.

As time advanced their love affair, Coop's health degenerated, and he became listless, almost emaciated. I tried to suggest to Lupe that they take a sabbatical from each other, telling her that Coop was not a well man and needed considerable rest.

We met on the studio lot, and as I spoke she kept tucking and twisting her blouse into the voluminous folds of her skirt. "No, Deek," she said with her thick Mexican accent as she shook her head. "Lupe has much love and heart for these quiet hombre," she assured me. Like all damsels caught up in an emotional jamboree, she felt she could not harm him. Coop went along. He loved Lupe as much as he was capable of loving. Naturally, it affected his career and his health, because Lupe lived by night. Her sexual drive took so much from him that he didn't have the strength to cope with both his work and Lupe.

I'll never forget my fears one night upon returning from the film stage to my dressing room. Of the many suites running from the entrance of the lot past the administration building and overlooking a small inside park, Coop's dressing room was the one at the very end.

---

36 Born in Mexico, she came to the United States and was acting in silent films by 1927. Known for her unfortunate love affairs, she would die in an unexplained suicide wearing full makeup and thus become a Hollywood urban legend (1908–1944).

As I walked toward my room, I noticed Coop's door ajar. I looked in and saw him stretched out on the floor, lifeless. I called out his name, and his eyelids flickered. His face was colorless, and I knelt beside him and asked, "What happened? Did you fall?"

He opened his eyes and stared blankly for a second until he recognized me, then he gave a half chuckle, whispered, "Too much homework," and passed out cold.

I phoned the studio doctor, and arrangements were quickly made to get him to the Presbyterian Hospital on Vermont and Sunset Boulevards, where the doctor would meet us. Coop was very ill with yellow jaundice, and it was to be a long time until he recovered. During his convalescence I visited him as often as I could, and his hospital room was filled with flowers from his many well-wishers. One day a magnificent floral arrangement arrived from Lupe, and as he handled the bouquet, he mused, "I will never understand, Dick, why they don't manufacture her type of body model in this country."

His doctors repeatedly warned him to conserve his energy, and he tried. Nevertheless, his experience did not curb Lupe's exuberance when he recovered, and the studio realized he had to get away from her. A few months later, Paramount transferred him to their eastern studio in Astoria, Long Island, to make *His Woman* (1931) with Claudette Colbert.[37]

Around that time the studio asked me if I would go to Astoria and make a closing picture for the year. I accepted. In fact, I was thrilled to go to New York and make a picture, as I had never made one in the East. Coop and I saw a lot of each other, and he told me he had met the Countess D'Frazzio[38] and her brother, Bert White. The

---
37 Born in France and a leading actress for two decades (1935–1968).
38 A wealthy American widow who had been married to a French count.

American-born countess had taken a liking to him and had invited him to accompany her and her brother on a safari in Africa.

Coop, the countess, and her brother left for Europe, from where they would embark to Africa around the Kenya area. Little did I realize he would be gone for almost nine months, but I corresponded with him and kept him informed on what was happening on my side of the ocean. Ironically, interest in Cooper grew after he affiliated himself with the countess. Instead of hurting his career, the publicity careened him to the top. Society columnists and magazine writers vied with each other for each new detail of his activities abroad, which impressed Paramount tremendously. He had become a glamorous legend, and housewives brushed aside the Home & Garden section to read about him. Coop's trip to Africa became his blooming period, his metamorphosis from deadpan cowboy to cosmopolitan lover.

After the trio left Africa, they went to Rome, where the countess took him to Carachini's, the finest men's clothier in that city, and outfitted him to perfection. The three worldly travelers then went on to London, where I sent him an SOS letter, urging him to get back to work. I wrote:

Dear Knothead,
    I'm glad for your sake you are bouncing around Europe and you have caused a near riot with your innumerable fans who miss you, but don't forget the public is fickle. Your one picture with Claudette Colbert was a success, but it won't carry you forever.

The rest of my letter was a gentle tirade about people who think they are better than others because they own Italian suits, the usual

Hollywood gossip concerning whose scalp was getting clipped, and a question about his vocabulary. Had it increased?

A few weeks later, I received a reply, which read:

Dear Dick,
Part One: Yup
Part Two: Nope

Yours sincerely, Coop

Within a short time, miraculously, and with great aplomb, a new personality embarked from a ship in New York and presented himself to Paramount as though he had only been away for five minutes. The studio bigwigs were overwhelmed with the distinguished figure who arrived in a bowler hat and Chesterfield coat, wearing a thin, silk umbrella over his arm. Coop had grown tremendously in poise and confidence. He was now most communicable.

Jack Moss, a former production manager at Paramount, took a good look at his eminence and immediately went to work as Coop's personal manager. Next, Elsa Maxwell, the famous socialite party giver, joined the countess's entourage and built Coop's image into one of a suave, fascinating man-about-town. It was then only a double-time step for Moss to execute some fancy footwork. Moss not only managed the gentleman's affairs; he extricated all of Coop's back salary from the studio, which he insisted had accumulated while Coop was in Africa, and acquired a tremendous increase in salary for the late bloomer.

The studios were forced to look at a Beau Brummel who had abandoned boots and cactus for colognes and cocktails. And then the incredible happened, and Coop got top billing in *Devil and the Deep* (1932) with Charles Laughton and Tallulah Bankhead.

I was working on a picture in Hollywood when I received a call from Coop telling me to meet his train in Pasadena. I was totally unprepared for his entrance. He stepped down on the depot platform wearing his black bowler hat, and instead of an umbrella, he carried a monkey on his arm.[39]

He stayed on as my houseguest for a few days, and my telephone rang constantly for him. One of the callers was Lupe, who had heard of his return. She wanted to see him. I had to tell her no, and she would say yes, and Coop refused to answer. She began to bombard my home with telephone calls.

We were sitting at dinner on the second evening of his visit, trading shop talk, when my butler announced, "You have a caller, Mr. Arlen." He pointed to a disheveled Lupe standing in my entry hall, her lovely hair disarranged, her face in a questioning expression. She walked toward the dining room where Coop was sitting and said, "You knew I would come to see you, Garee."

Coop nodded and took her hand, saying, "How did you get in here, little mountain goat?"

I was thinking along the same lines, because I had an electric gate that provided no admittance and a seven-foot wall on all sides of the house, which she would have had to scale.

Coop spoke to her very tenderly, as he didn't want to hurt her any more than he already had, and Lupe, protesting her intense love for him, managed to calm herself. I left the two of them alone to talk things

---

39 A la John Barrymore, who was famous for this.

over. Later that evening, Coop told me she had realized their romance was over and had taken their final parting well. Sweet Lupe, I don't think to her dying day she ever loved anyone else but Gary Cooper.

He moved out of my house and rented a mansion in Brentwood. Coop hired a staff of servants, including a chauffeur for his Duesenberg and Cadillac cars. He resided in his hillside aerie in an aura of baronial splendor. Elsa Maxwell and the countess took over his social life and initiated a whirl of parties that never fewer than a hundred guests attended.

I was invited to a dinner party and was stunned seeing Coop in this opulent environment. Each party was better than the one before. One evening I had to use his private bathroom, and in order to get there, I had to pass through his dressing room. I glanced around his expensively decorated bedroom and at his bed, the size of a dance floor. On top of his imported Vicuna bedspread lay two huge Afghan hounds. I left late in the evening. I thought of the imported dogs, imported spats and canes, imported titled guests, imported countess, and all the exotic props he had collected to create a sensational scene. He got a kick out of all of it.

He knew before he returned to Hollywood that he was to make a picture with Tallulah Bankhead. This did not sit too well with the countess, as she was afraid Coop might become enamored with the US senator's daughter. He promised to be good, and the countess then obliged by naming his pet monkey Tallulah. I cautioned him on this, as Tallulah was a lovely lady; the whole thing was ridiculous. He agreed, and we changed the monkey's name to Toluca, after my home in Toluca Lake. The press loved it.

Coop was now a full-fledged movie-star idol. His main problem at this time was that he could not obtain certain pictures he wished to make at Paramount. He purposely let his contract lapse and then went to see Sam Goldwyn to further his career. I felt that when Coop left Paramount, it was a break of the old guard consisting of Jack Oakie,[40] Buddy Rogers, and me. We had been the mainstays of the studio. Richard Dix[41] had left because I supplanted him. He went to RKO and won an Academy Award for playing the part of Yancy in *Cimarron*. In spite of Coop's move to MGM, we continued to see each other.

Coop's father, like mine, had been a judge in the Supreme Court.[42] This background drew us together. We felt parallels in our lives in such interests as sports, travel, music, and the arts. One of Coop's unique talents was drawing. He could sketch anything. Some of his pen and inks were extraordinary. He designed all the costumes he wore on the screen, putting in touches he thought would be good for the characters he portrayed. When color films came in, he knew how to blend hues that were right for the roles he played. While waiting for takes on the set, he would draw the crew in detail on the back pages of his script.

His best drawings were those of animals. At that time I owned a boat. We sailed to San Diego and anchored at beautiful Glorietta Bay. Coop had this magnificent feeling and love for animals. Morning after morning we would head for the zoo.

On our way to the animals' playpen, I would ask Coop, "Think we should look in on your friend?"

Coop would grin and say, "Sure."

---

40   American actor (1903–1978).
41   Silent and sound star (1893–1949) known for rugged hero parts.
42   Richard's father was a Supreme Court justice in Minnesota. Gary Cooper's father was a Supreme Court justice in Montana.

Then we would head for the gorilla's cage. The ape sat impatiently, waiting for Coop. When he saw him, he would make the strangest cooing, breathing sounds. The two were fascinated with each other. Coop would walk up to his cage and take his paw, and the gorilla would kiss his hand and put his face up against the bars to be petted.

Another pet of his was a wild eagle. Though others could rarely get near him, Coop had a special sleeve made and trained the bird to sit tranquilly on his arm while he fed him.

I have always believed that any man who had the quality or inner spirit to make animals love him had to be different from ordinary humans. Even to his last days when he was dying from cancer,[43] there were no complaints from Coop. In fact, I never heard him complain at any time about anything. Nor did I ever hear him say an unkind word. If anyone made a snide remark about someone, he would remain silent, and if one put a direct question to him about this particular person, he would say, "I always found him to be a nice person." Then he would chuckle to himself, "Isn't that about right?"

---

[43] Cooper died in 1961 from both lung and prostate cancers.

The Thirties

Recollections of Toluca Lake and Breezy Top

Now and again I miss the TV program showing my Toluca Lake home, which was narrated and filmed by Ken Murray (1950). I have been told he played this half hour quite a few times. *Wings* gave me the money to build this wonderful house.

The house was built in the early 1930s. It was a beautiful twenty-room house facing Toluca Lake, with a boat dock and a long lawn where I practiced my golf shots along the stone fence built by Allan Ladd when he was a mason, some years before he became an actor. In fact, it was before Susan, his wife, became his agent and catapulted his career to stardom. I loved that home, not only because it was annexed to Lakeside Country Club, but also because I took pride in the Toluca Lake area, which was really a land development created by Bing Crosby, Bob Hope, and me.

We decided to make an "ultra-real-estate development." Because of certain conditions, we were not able to carry out our plans, and we were floundering like a swamp. A bunch of us got together and cleaned the "actual swamp"[44] and took all the debris out, dredged it,

---

[44] It began as a natural, spring-fed, swampy pond and was enhanced into a six-acre water feature for the planned neighborhood (from the *History of Toluca Lake* by the Chamber of Commerce).

and stocked it with fish and kept it clean. We put flagstone walls up all around the property and made it level. Then the stock-market crash occurred. I took over a lot of property so the fellows wouldn't lose credit. I kept so much of it for friends with certain specifications by the Toluca Lake Association, which was organized in 1934.

Those friends included film stars W. C. Fields, Bob Hope, Ann Blyth, Bing Crosby, Frank Sinatra, and Mary Astor.

However, my marriage was not working out with my second wife, Jobyna Ralston, whom I starred with in *Wings*. When the divorce ended in 1946, I gave her the house and then built the house in Breezy Top.

I gave her more than the house. There was considerable real estate, cash, and much more. In fact, I gave her the *Jobyna II*, bought in 1930 and named for her around 1936. I kept the boat moored at Avalon at Catalina and spent many enjoyable hours aboard her. The boat was forty-eight feet long and forty-seven feet wide, and it was built by Stanton, Reed & Hibbbard in Los Angeles in 1926. It belonged originally to Walter Houston, and he transferred it to me in 1930.[45] It was during this period that he lived in my guesthouse in Toluca Lake for one year as he went through a nasty divorce.

Well, our son, Rick, was then only three years old, and I was torn apart in leaving him and dissolving our marriage. But circumstances led up to this chapter in my life, and when the domestic situation was unbearable, we parted.

---

45 Houston changed the name to *Jobyna-Nan* in 1930 and transferred the title, but by 1936 the official name was *Jobyna II* according to Lloyd's registry of yachts.

A Boat Called *Jobyna* and Harry Cohn

~

THE BOAT BROUGHT SEVERAL VERY interesting experiences into my life. As I began to learn, one of the problems with being under contract to a major studio was their power to refuse to loan an actor to another studio if he was a valuable property. Paramount would not loan me to Metro to do *Inspiration* (1931) with Garbo. The picture won accolades as an Academy Award nominee and would have been a feather in my cap.

Columbia wanted me for *Dirigible* (1931) and *Flight* (1931), and I couldn't accept. Paramount would not allow me to make *Holiday* (1931), another Academy nominee. So, I left Paramount and went to Columbia, which was run by the czar, Harry Cohn (1891–1958). It was my misfortune at this time that Cohn and Darryl Zanuck were feuding. Cohn, under no circumstances, would allow me to make a picture for 20th Century Fox. During this time, I wasn't working or making any pictures at Columbia, and 20th Century offered to pay a $50,000 bonus plus the loan of a well-known star to Columbia in exchange for my services to make *Rebecca of Sunnybrook Farm* (1938) with Shirley Temple.[46] I lost out to the two moguls who

---

46 Shirley would become a famous child star from this picture (1928–2014).

were clashing over policy and because Columbia refused to consider my interests.

In the meantime, Mrs. Temple asked me if I knew of some nice actor for Shirley to work together with, as she was very fussy with people, especially actors, with whom Shirley came in contact. I suggested a friend of mine who was an able performer, but who, in despair of making it with his career, had left to return to his home in North Carolina.

Upon my suggestion, the studio contacted Randolph Scott. Scott returned to a brand-new career and a lucrative contract at 20th Century. He made one successful picture after another. He prospered and went into business with Nat Holt and Harry Jo Brown for RKO Studios (Radio Keith Orpheum). He became a multimillionaire and retired, and I doubt, to this day, if he knows I referred him for the role opposite Shirley Temple.

I knew what I had lost, and I blamed Cohn. One day I was on my boat at Catalina Harbor. Cohn had his own boat and came over without an invitation to my boat and asked my skipper, Walter, "Is it all right to come on this actor's boat?"[47] This statement was the way Cohn showed contempt for actors, although he was dependent on them for his livelihood. I sat in the bow and saw Cohn but didn't move forward to greet him. So, when Cohn again shouted his request, Walter answered, "Mr. Arlen is a yachtsman and a gentleman, and you will have to ask him."

---

47 Cohn was known to treat actors like chattel.

I shouted to Cohn, "Get off my boat, you damned jerk, and don't use any of your foul language around here.[48] One more foot on deck, and I will paste your nose on your eyes," I threatened.

I reminded Cohn of the Temple picture, and just as surely as Cohn had been surly one minute, he suddenly became contrite and admitted that he was wrong.

One thing Cohn did do was to suddenly own up to his foul acts, which left you speechless, as it took all the fight out of you. Cohn used this contriteness and often displayed it in his dealings, thereby reversing the situation. "I was wrong, and I admit it," Cohn would say, which was fair enough. Only the SOB took so long—like months—in admitting his error that I wanted to splay his wide nose with a left hook. It was too late for the picture

During this period of disappointments Dick was cast as the male lead in an unusal science fiction horror picture. This movie would eventually bring him more fame than "Wings".

Island of Lost Souls

In 1932 Paramount produced "Island of Lost Souls". The movie was based on H.G. Well's controversial book about the theory of evolution. Charles Laughton would create the world's greatest sadist conducting experiments on animals and humans. Bela Lugosi was equally hirsute as the unforgettable Beast Man, "Sayer of the Law". Dick was cast in the lead as a shipwrecked sailor forced to stay on Moreau's isolated South Sea island until help could come for him. Dr. Moreau saves him from drowning. He quickly discovers his sinister reasons for doing so and realizes he must escape. Moreau's

---

48 Mom's notes: Dick once told her that Cohn had his nose plastered all over his face from the fights he had lost.

downfall will come from his own creatures in revenge for his experiments upon them.

As the years went by the movie developed a great following. It is now known as a "cult" movie. Though "PG" the movie remains as frightening now due to Lugosi and Laughton's marvelous acting as it was over 80 years ago. Dick and Laughton began a friendship during the course of the movie which remained until Charles died.

The Forties

Breezy Top

I bought some forty-odd acres out in the country, virgin land with a stream running through it from the dam, which was built to contain the lake.

As previously mentioned, I must be near water, even if it is a water fountain, just to feel the cool, healing strength of it and watch its ceaseless action. Even calm water moves with the slightest breeze.

On top of the highest bluff, I built Breezy Top, covering 3,500 square feet, a many-winged house pivoted around the living- and dining-room area. The servants' quarters housed my houseman, Leander, and his wife, Aileen. They were a marvelous couple who had come up from the South—Kentucky, I believe—and took pride in their responsibility of running the house, as much of the time I was an absentee owner, either on location filming a picture or abroad.

Both Leander and his wife were very particular about guests in the house, especially houseguests who did not know their place. Leander was overseer of the place, and Aileen's domicile encircled the huge kitchen with built-in everything, from an open pit oven to the room-sized walk-in freezer. We hung our own meats from the farm and had the refrigerated cupboards stocked with a year's supply of perishables. This was necessary as we were far out from the city and shopping. I had a number of hands that worked and lived on the grounds. I loved to entertain impromptu and have forty guests for dinner on short notice, to which Leander and wife responded like troupers.

They, too, shared in the fun and kidding by my friends who came over to the ranch and enjoyed the casual life we led. There was always a well-stocked liquor supply and some of the best drinkers in town, but nobody ever got out of hand.

The Gabor Sisters

In May 1967, a paragraph appeared in Walter Winchell's syndicated column, from which I quote verbatim:

> You rarely read stories about the Gabor Sisters like this one… Richard Arlen, long time handsome movie star, met Zsa Zsa and Eva shortly after they first arrived in Girlywood…They were broke…he loaned them a sizeable sum…One day the Dolls invited the benefactor over for dinner…after the feast (and the laughs) they presented him with a cigarette case… inside was the total sum he had loaned them…six $1,000 bills…[49]

The ellipses were Winchell's. I have no idea as to the source of this material or why it was ever printed, and I hope the girls will not take offense at my little reminiscences. I give tremendous credit to these two beautiful women who have taken their lumps and given same in return. They have always been fair in their dealings, straight down center plate. The Gabors come on strong, like scintillating astral bodies; although I must admit when I first met them, they were not, at least to me, exactly heaven-sent.

---

[49] Dick was now taking small parts in B and C movies. The Gabors were wealthy and repaid Dick, known for his kindness and generosity, as very few ever did.

I met Eva in 1941 in Hollywood. She had fled Hungary to become an actress in this country, and having some influential friends in Hollywood, she followed their advice to try and get into a Richard Arlen movie. I was then starring in *Forced Landing* for Paramount.

One later afternoon during a break, I returned to my dressing room bungalow for a necessary catnap from the daily grind. When I entered my quarters, I discovered her waiting for me. In spite of my obvious annoyance, she made no move to leave. Nobody said a word, and so I opened the door for her. Now, having made this broad gesture, I stood at the door and began to feel like an imbecile. Eva did not move but merely shrugged and flipped her soft, blond hair, smiled with a slow, feline grace, and in that foreign accent, the Gabor trademark, purred, "I vant to make a picture with you."

That voice! I wanted to swing from the chandelier, and I asked her, "What have you done in pictures?"

"Nothing."

"Nothing?"

"No." She shook her head. Then she sweetly answered, "But I am here now."

By the end of the afternoon, I told Eva to see the head of wardrobe, and I gave her the leading role opposite mine, as I had the final word in casting. When we next met on the set, she asked, "Vat do I have to do now?"

I replied, "Nothing."

I told her just to learn her craft, and she would be fine. And I meant it. She had something special in her enthusiasm and her sense of timing, traits that are difficult to learn. Moreover, she had a feminine resilience that would serve her well in our competitive jungle.

Several weeks after completion of *Forced Landing*, she appeared on the set where I was making a new picture, *Flying Blind* (1941). I was at the top of the stage, forty feet up, when Eva called to me.

"Yoo-hoo. Come down here."

"Can't," I replied, "I'm busy."

"For a second, come down, or you miss a surprise." She had brought her sister, Zsa Zsa, then known as Madame Belge, wife of the Turkish foreign minister of propaganda, and wanted to introduce me to her. After the introductions, Zsa Zsa smiled warmly. She spoke little English, but I could see a friendly look in her eyes.

"You good to my sister," she told me, "so I love you too."

The three of us maintained a good relationship. There was a third sister, Magda, who retired early from her acting involvements.

In Hungary, the sisters had lived in better-than-average circumstances with pap, Peter, a jeweler (five stores), and mam, Madame Jolie, an adhesive and polarizing influence in her beautiful daughters' careers. Zsa Zsa married young and had all the material advantages but was not content to remain the wife of a diplomat many years older than herself. When she visited this country, she decided to stay permanently, as she felt she could contribute to the industry as an actress.

Unhappily for the Gabors, the Hungarian government would not permit them, as they were Jewish, to bring their money or family jewels here. They fled the Nazis and arrived first in Portugal and finally the United States, penniless. This meant they had to establish themselves quickly in order to survive on this continent.

One night the telephone rang at my Northridge ranch. A breathless, feminine voice spoke, "Muzeeka, you guess who iss calling you?"

As only the Gabors used this Hungarian term of endearment, I pretended ignorance.

"Iss Eva and Zsa Zsa, dahling." She pronounced it Ava. I could hear Zsa Zsa in the background. There was conversation going on between the girls in their native tongue at their end of the line. It sounded like a disagreement.

Then Eva returned to tell me, "So, ve are having troubles, dahling."

There followed a long, explanatory dialogue, which I interrupted several times to comprehend. It all boiled down to their eviction from their apartment for lack of funds. They had nowhere to go, and they had come to me for assistance.

This was followed by much laughter, giggles, and more entreaties for help. They didn't seem to be suffering. However, I rang off and sent my driver, Leander, to pick them up. They became my houseguests for an unspecified time.

Within twenty-four hours, my home became a Hungarian goulash. Every friend or cousin found my address. The Gabors were a gregarious lot, and I had a well-stocked pantry and liquor cellar. Everything was fine until my servants threatened to leave.

One day I told the girls, "I'm sorry. Things are a little hectic here, and the staff is tired of listening to the gypsy rhapsody. They're just not used to this type of composition."

Zsa Zsa agreed. "But dahling, ov course ve dun't vant to upset you, so dun't vorry." They told me of a nice house in the country their relatives had suggested they might rent, a former health resort.

A few hours later, after the last sliced onion had been left to mold on my upholstered chairs, they piled into my car with their belongings. We drove for hours until nightfall, when we found the place we were looking for—a broken-down shack somewhere in the tullies. It had the cheerful mien of Wuthering Heights. Not a soul was on the grounds, and the house looked like it had been beaten to death. A brass bed headboard hung halfway out of one broken window, and weeds had climbed through another. I never saw such dejected faces as theirs.

In unison they cried, "Vat a horrible place!"

There was no point in going inside. It was late, and we were tired. I turned my car around and drove them to my boat, *The Pagan*, a sixty-five-foot schooner anchored in Newport Harbor. The girls were thrilled. I had my misgivings, as the Newport Yacht Club was composed of strictly conservative members with pedigreed names. I didn't mind losing my membership, but there were rules to observe. Never have I been so wrong.

"We love it, Muzeeka," they trilled. The following day they found the club locker room, emerging in the briefest bathing suits ever seen on that purist beach. They ran around full of life, and the members took them to their hearts. Not so my skipper. When Walt saw me coming aboard with my entourage, he almost rang up the distress flag. He and the crew had just refinished the teakwood decks and had painted and varnished the schooner until she glistened. When the girls sighted my well-stocked galley, they screamed, "Lunch!" Picnic operations immediately began on the rear deck. Then, when they really set up housekeeping and flung their laundry over the fore boom to dry, I left and went back to my ranch.

Two days later Walt called me with a list of complaints and tactful suggestions as to my choice in dismissing my skipper or my guests. I was working on my film, *Flying Blind*, and couldn't leave the studio. I sent an emissary, who reported that the skipper was ready to slash his throat. Just when I thought of putting the girls to sea in a rowboat filled with a cargo of salamis, word came that Eva's option had been taken up by her studio. At the time, I did not know that the whole Gabor family was living off the small salary she brought in, and that her contract was in jeopardy of not being renewed. From then on they established themselves as recognized actresses.

In 1944 I went to New York to discuss *Too Hot for Maneuvers*, an upcoming play for the following year that I was to be in. Mr. Hilton was in the process of taking over the Plaza, and by coincidence we both took the same train back to Los Angeles. At the time, I had a presentiment that his marriage to Zsa Zsa[50] wasn't going too well. I had been a spectator, along with Eva, when we'd joined the engaged couple for dinner on several occasions. I was really amazed when they married. I couldn't help noticing how engrossed Mr. Hilton was with his various business enterprises, which left Zsa Zsa to her own resources.

---

50 Zsa Zsa Gabor was married nine times.

In 1945 I did the play in New York. I arrived at the Plaza Hotel, where I stayed for the duration of the play, a four-month run. There, lo and behold, I ran into Zsa Zsa Gabor, now married to Conrad Hilton, who owned the hotel.

On several occasions I saw the girls in the Plaza lobby. I was terribly busy with my play and did not have any time for social functions, so we did not get together.[51]

Five years later, in 1950, I was visiting New York and ran into Eva, who was getting good notices and triumphing in a play called *The Happy Time*. Eva insisted I attend a matinee performance.

As I walked toward the theater, I looked up at the marquee. There was Eva's name in bright, flashing lights. Now I know it takes many, many years for the majority of actors to play on Broadway (at least at that time). Many marvelous performers have never even made it. Nevertheless, here, in all her burnished glory, was the middle Gabor girl with one little motion-picture credit to her name in *Forced Landing* (1941), and it was not a particularly good picture. And I didn't feel she was any closer to an Academy Award than when we had made that picture some years back. No matter, Eva had a great deal of charm, the play was a success, and that is all one needs.

I would run into Eva one more time, years later in the sixties, when I was working on an episode of *Petticoat Junction*[52] with Buddy Rogers. The story was about the return of two World War II aviators to Hootersville. Ed Buchanan, who plays the girls' uncle, had been waiting forty years for our return, and when we finally arrived in a vintage motorcar, the whole town turned out to celebrate.

---

51 Eva is now married to her second husband, Charles Isaac, and will marry three more times.
52 TV series, which ran from 1963 to 1970.

All the performers of *Petticoat Junction*, *Beverly Hillbillies*, and *Green Acres* rehearsed on stages next to each other. While waiting to perform, I felt a tap on my shoulder and turned around to see the lovely Eva of *Green Acres*,[53] a ravishing creature expensively rigged in a feather-and-chiffon peignoir, not exactly the farmer's wife.

"Muzeeka! Ha!"

"Eva?"

"Dahling, I have missed you."

She leaned over to Irene Ryan, whom I was sitting next to, and exclaimed, "I have always been in luv with Richard." I was thrilled. "He iss such old friend."

"Eva," I asked, "did you see my show?"

"But ov course, dahling."

I repeated all my funny lines, awaiting her reaction. "Remember when Buddy and I arrive in Hootersville and the country storekeeper thinks he recognizes us and tells his wife, 'Here is Clive Brooks and Monte Blue, come to visit us.'" I collapsed with the recollection of the screams of amusement that line drew. Then I watched her puzzled face.

"Clive Brooks and Monte Blue," I repeated.

"So vat, dahling? Vat is Clive Brook and Monte Blue?"

"They were two other guys, see?" I felt betrayed.

---

53 TV series, which ran from 1965 to 1971.

"So vat did they do?"

"So, so nothing. So vat?" I said.

She did not even know the part I had played, but she caressed my hair, kissed me, and went off.

Well, so what…those two sisters parlayed their respective fortunes and kept those wonderful accents forevermore, which is part of their lovely mystery. Who else can peel off "Muzeeka" and make it sound like the tinkle of small bells ringing in the wind?

A short time ago,[54] I revisited Breezy Top. It was like visiting a ghost town. The subdividers had hacked away a place of beauty and whittled it down to small lots. The roads were gone, as was the beautiful white fence that led up the main drive and along the horse corrals. The barn was gone, having been burned down some time back. The house was there, paint peeling, run down, with large plots of weeds where former gardens had been carefully tended for cutting arrangements for the house. It was so neglected by its present owners that only a skeletal part of its beauty remained. I had planted an avenue of olive trees to stretch from the rear end of the house down the gradual slope until they reached street level. Some of these trees had been destroyed or died from lack of care until they looked like a ravaged line of scraggy plants, the kinds of trees left after a blitzkrieg in war-torn countries. The tightly clipped grass lawn covering a wide expanse around the house had grown to waist-high weeds.

I used to get up at dawn and look out my bedroom window, enchanted with the sun rising on acres of green valley, and watch and hear the sheep and cattle as they were led out of the barn. I enjoyed the pastoral picture of horses leaving the stables, the dogs dogging

---
54   In the forties Dick had attempted to create a farming business.

their heels. I had a penchant for St. Bernard dogs for some reason, and at one time I had twenty of them boarding at the ranch. There was plenty of room for them, so why not give them a home?

Now, as I looked around, all the boundaries were gone. I stood on the highest level of the hill and looked around for a landmark or a familiar object. All I could discover was the stone marker where the dam had been. Gone were the orange trees, the groves of trees I had planted when I went into the business of farming. This project took place in World War II. The soil was so rich and the terrain so perfect for drainage that I had selected the Valencia oranges for a commercial venture.

At night one could smell the heady fragrance of the orange blossoms that swept that part of the country, as all my neighbors had orange groves, and when the trees are blooming, there is almost a sensual bouquet in the air.

I drove around the new streets that had been hacked out of the hills and the modern houses, typical suburbia, but rather nice, still looking for a part of my past other than a rotted end of a fence post. I came out on Devonshire Boulevard, turned right to a big, mounted billboard announcing "Porter Ranch," and continued on.

Further up the boulevard, I saw a border of tall cypress trees, a double row leading up to an old French château house that used to belong to Robert Taylor.

At that time he was a young and vital star and a wealthy bachelor keeping company with a young actress who had a ranch down the road. Her name was Barbara Stanwyck, and she later became Mrs. Taylor.

Ahh, the Black Widow, as we called her. At one time on Devonshire and Tampa, there was a beautiful estate that housed a beautiful dame. She was truly magnificent, with beautiful, black hair and a sexy body, barely thirty years old. Bob Taylor and I would drive by and comment on the type of maintenance men she hired to do the gardening and drive her cars. They looked more like bodyguards than field hands. And that was what they were. One day Bob and I stopped at the one grocery store in the village to get some supplies, and the owner was counting his money in his till, sniffing it and counting it, and Bob asked, "What in the blazes are you up to?" Which was an intelligent question, as the old man was completely concentrated on his nose. Finally, the old buck looked up and said to us, "Smell this money."

He had sorted the bills into separate piles. "Violet perfume," he pointed to one stack. "This un's more like heliotrope, and 'un's like lily of the valley," and he went on enumerating the various odors.

He stopped momentarily from his count and looked at us as he told us that the gorgeous gal we admired had just stopped by to pay her grocery bill, all in cash. He emphasized that she always paid in cash, even though her account often amounted to a thousand dollars or more. Each time the money smelled like floral perfumes.

Bob and I looked at each other and came to the same conclusion. Our fair damsel ran a sporting house and had a lot of boarders to feed on her ranch. Each time a girl got paid off, she placed her booty in her bosom, which was well saturated with scent. As she paid a portion of her take to the boss, it would literally stink of her cologne. This money paid the bills, and the old man was caught in his own thoughts and visions of what had taken place.

Would the countryside ever seem the same to me again?

The Fifties

LAUREL AND HARDY

IN 1953 I WENT TO do two films for Charles Deane Productions at Ealing Studios.⁵⁵ One picture was *Devil's Harbor* with Greta Gynt.⁵⁶ Unfortunately, the other one escapes me.

Arrangements had been made ahead at either the Savoy or the Dorchester. When I arrived at the hotel, the clerk nodded a greeting and said, "So glad to have you with us, Mr. Arlen. Mr. Laurel and Mr. Hardy are stopping with us too." Now that was an unexpected surprise.

I knew the boys had played all over the continent before bringing their show to the Hammersmith Theater,⁵⁷ which is on the outskirts of London; but until then, I hadn't known where they were staying. Oliver (Babe) Hardy, Stan Laurel, and I had been friends since the early twenties. Babe, as he was called, and I were members of Lakeside Golf Club in Toluca Lake, California, where we played golf regularly. It was great to find somebody from home.

---

55 Ealing began in 1902 and is still in business today.
56 Glamorous Norwegian actress, 1917–2000.
57 Originally known as the Gaumont Palace, it opened its doors in 1932. It seats 3,500 people.

Stan Laurel was born in England and made his home in Los Angeles; Oliver Hardy lived in a five-acre ranch house in the San Fernando Valley, where Horace Heidt, the former bandleader, lived on his multiacre Country Club Estates.

The English love their royalty and their superstars. They had bestowed a moniker on the two comedians: "The Thin Man and the Fat Man," a title paid in absolute homage, eulogizing the two princes of mirth and humor who gave them so much pleasure. They were fabulously funny men.

Offstage they were as different as the characters they portrayed. Babe was extremely sensitive, as many heavy people are. He was a positive person, a good man as well as artist, immaculate to the double nth degree, and surprisingly a graceful dancer as well as an outstanding golfer. Stan was rather frail, and though he took pride in his appearance, his hair had the unkempt effect of having been tousled in a wind tunnel. He was a practical man who did not always defer to his partner's judgment, nor did he call the large one by his nickname of "Babe." It was Ollie. "Ollie, what do you think of this situation?" Having juxtaposing traits, they cohesively worked together on the same wavelengths. They fed each other lines as easily as feeding coins in a slot machine. And they managed to come up with some bumper jackpots.

It was no surprise, in view of the high esteem in which they were held, that the English considered it most trivial to travel fifteen miles out of London to see their favorites cavort on stage. At the time I came to London, the boys had just finished a run at the Palladium Theatre[58] in the heart of that city; yet their devoted fans made the trip to the Hammerstein repeatedly. The two comics were the most popular artists to ever hit the continent. Prior to coming

---

58   Opened in 1910 and still going strong, it seats 2,286 people.

to England, they had made personal appearances in Italy, France, Norway, Sweden, and Denmark, and they had done their entire routines in pantomime, packing the houses at every performance. The Hammersmith was no different.

As soon as I checked in to my hotel rooms, I phoned Babe in his suite. He was as happy as I to get together and said, "Stan is out, Dick. You go down to the grill and wait for me, and I will buy you a drink."

When I arrived downstairs, he was sitting at a table and had already ordered my usual drink. We chatted about America, the film industry, and friends. Then I asked, "What kind of act are you doing at the Hammersmith?"

He paused, his round eyes blinking, and said, "I really couldn't tell you, because it changes every night. We improvise as we go along."

He suggested I come to the theater if I wasn't too busy. About six thirty that night, his Rolls-Royce, flanked with footman and chauffeur, pulled up to our hotel. Mrs. Hardy, Mrs. Laurel, a friend of theirs, Babe, and I got into the car and left for the Hammersmith. In England at that time, the custom was to omit the matinee performance and do two evening shows.

At seven thirty, the curtain went up, and I have never in my life heard such earsplitting applause, foot stomping, whooping, and cheers in staid Great Britain. The ovation lasted three minutes, and finally the play began.

The howling audience, who knew the player's routines, waited breathlessly for any changes in their act. Their popularity was created by their ability to throw away the script and create an improvised show from their wild imaginations. Suddenly, with urbane dignity and positive misdirection, they would conjure a mishmash of delightful quality and run it through to a glorious finish. The fat imp and the thin imp.

The night I attended as their guest, the scene for the first act was an operating room in a hospital.[59] Instruments of torture hung on the walls along with bedpans, knives, and a few family portraits framed in sterile white. The operating table was dead center. Babe was the doctor and Stan the patient.

Dr. Hardy, fingering a saw, would glance over at the cringing patient stretched out on the table and assure him, "This won't hurt a bit if you are careful and do everything I say."

Stan would cry, raise the sheet to hide his quivering face and hat, and say, "Ollie, I think I'm going to be sick."

"Now, Stanley, you must be brave. Remember, a stitch in time..."

The doctor kept up a steady monologue to soothe his patient, meanwhile assiduously dropping instruments on the floor, which had to be picked up by an attractive young nurse in a miniskirt before minis were worn. As the act continued, the operation focused more on the nurse than on the patient, with the dialogue and action shifting until, with the dexterity of a magician, the patient and nurse changed places, and she ended up on the table. The boys knew that night that one of their best boosters from the United States was sitting out front, and so they turned everything loose. The act lasted forty minutes overtime. The audience was screaming with laughter, the manager of the house yelling with pain.

---

59 Absolute burlesque.

After the show Babe gave me that toodle-de-do hand wave and said, "Come join us at the pub."

Everybody in England has their favorite pub, and the boys had theirs. When we arrived, every stouthearted lass and lad in the place received the thin one and the fat one with open arms. Those two never turned down a drink.

I had made a film called *The Four Feathers* (1929)[60] some years previously. The picture had been filmed in England and was a historic film eulogizing the brave youth of Great Britain in the early days of the Boer War. The picture had taken almost a year to make, and because the English never forget you, I had my own cortege of well-wishers. It was good to receive recognition, and I drank glass for glass, accepting their toasts until it was time to return to the theater for the second show. Meanwhile, the management had cleaned out the audience from the first show so that they couldn't stay for free. What followed was amazing. In the first performance, there were 3,500 viewers and standees; in the second review, they doubled the number of standees. I'm sure many people paid to come back the second time.

From somewhere the manager appeared and said, "Mr. Richard Arlen is with us this evening. Will you please come forward, Mr. Richard Arlen." I found myself on the stage taking a bow, and as I turned to leave, Stan grabbed me on one side and Babe on the other.

"We could use an able assistant here," said Babe, as he patted me on my back and helped me slip into a white jacket, thus bringing an unsuspecting and slightly inebriated American boy into their act. There is a certain routine in comedy. You know what the key is, and you follow it, and it isn't very hard to manage. You ad-lib because you

---

60 One of the last great "silent" epics. Dick was the star.

know what the procedure is, and so you go along with it. However, with these two zanies, the act became chaos.

"Please pick up your broom and get to work," Stan fumbled, looking to Ollie for confirmation. When I held the broom, they thought I was too weak to handle it. Before long, they had both the nurse and me on the operating table, where they performed a dual operation. I think the show ran about an hour and a half. I swear I have never heard a more hysterical audience.

I think one of the most amusing incidents that ever happened to Laurel and Hardy occurred during the days of prohibition. Later, the boys used this bit in one of their pictures. One day they phoned and invited me to their hideaway apartment on Washington Boulevard, near the Roach Studios in Los Angeles. They made pictures for Hal Roach[61] (1892–1992) and released them through MGM. When I arrived, they greeted me at the door with "Now, don't tell our wives and give away our little secret about this apartment, will you, Richard?" They pressed a glass of spiked near beer into my hands from an overloaded icebox.

As I sat drinking with them, they told me they were making some wine that day. The place smelled like a brewery. I heard the lids on the pots going ploppity-plop from the fermenting process, and the two of them took turns inspecting their concoction. Babe would come back from the kitchen, clasping his pudgy fingers, and say, "It's only a matter of time." Stan, savoring his glass of spirits, would echo, "It's only a matter of time." I had told them beforehand that I had another engagement, and so I left soon after their millionth round trip to the scullery, with a warning to watch their cooking. The rest is history published in our local papers.

---

61 American film and TV producer, director, and actor of the nineties, best known for *Laurel and Hardy* and the *Our Gang* film comedy series.

The weather outside was so inclement that the boys made themselves comfortable by stripping down to their shorts. This was years before air conditioning. Babe had lifted the lid on a kettle when sudden combustion from the gasses formed and blew out the entire front wall of the apartment building. Bricks, smashed windows, pieces of wood, and what was left of the place landed below on Washington Boulevard. The two comedians stood on the open second floor now exposed to the public, Babe in his blue shorts and Stan in a polka-dot number, their secret hideaway blown to bits.

They incorporated this incident into a film called *Boys Night Out*. In a scene from the picture, the men and their wives are together in a living room. It is evident the boys have been gallivanting a bit, and the wives are suspicious. Stan is sitting high up on a tall chair back of the davenport, and both wives are staring at Ollie, who has just told a convincing lie, saying the two husbands had attended the Orpheum Theatre on their night out and that they were perfectly innocent.

Stan's wife asks, "What was on the bill?"

Stan, sitting up higher than the others, has a newspaper in his hands. He turns to the entertainment section showing various types of acts appearing locally, including jugglers, acrobats, singers, and pantomimes to Ollie, who then confidently transmits these reports to two stony-eyed women. After a lengthy dissertation, Ollie smiles at the wives and says, "So, you see, my dears, we really were there." Stan agrees, his face bathed in his homely smirk, and turns the newspaper over to where the headlines scream, "Orpheum Theatre Burns to the Ground."

When the wives see the headlines, they start after the truants and give chase. Ollie's large wife reaches into a closet, gets a shotgun, and fires into the air. The camera pans to show forty guys in various stages of undress running for their lives from the apartment building.

The two comics figured out every routine they used in their pictures. When they went to work in the morning, they only had a thin story line. They hired several gagmen with unusual talents, but they were their own best writers. Each day they would leave for location with everything they planned to use on their truck, including their famous breakaway clothes.

Another great gag was the one with their car. The guy in front hit their bumper, and Laurel backed up, hitting the car in the rear. Then, the guy behind got mad and hit the car back of him. Soon the cars began to multiply until there were four blocks of wrecked cars. They took this same routine on shipboard. Laurel's hat blew off, and a guy laughed, so he took the man's hat and threw it away, and soon everybody on shipboard was throwing passengers' hats into the ocean.

I recall one routine concerning a house built around a tree. They planted some fertilizer underneath the tree; the next morning they were six stories in the air.

We were wonderful friends over the years, playing golf, talking shop, or gagging it up. One of their specialties was pulling gags on their gagmen. There was one particular gagman on their payroll whom they kept for inside laughs. They would bait him, and he would take the lure and run, getting himself into a corner acting out his joke. He would work himself into paroxysms of hysterics, tears coursing down his face from the intoxicating joys of creation. When he would finish, he'd look around for his employers, who had disappeared. Then Babe would reappear and signal to him, "Do it again, Charlie; we missed you."[62]

They will be missed.

---

[62] Oliver Hardy died of a stroke in 1957, and Stan Laurel died of a heart attack in 1965.

The Sixties[63]

HOLLYWOOD AND VINE! I WAS on a lecture tour in St. Louis, Missouri,[64] and had a few hours to kill. I rented a car and stopped at a rural gasoline station. A seedy, middle-aged attendant pointed his toothpick at me and said, "Recognized you, Mr. Arlen. You sure are a long way from California. Never been out there myself, but I sure would like to take the missus and see all the movie stars." He filled the gas tank, thought a bit, and popped the question at me, the question I've been asked so many times: "Say, what's it like at Hollywood and Vine?"

I could tell from his expression that the very thought of those famous streets meant a deluxe route of escapism to the land of beautiful starlets and Rolls-Royce cars.

I sat in the car wondering what to say, because I just didn't want to explode his dreams and tell him it was a commercial crossroad, the same he'd find in any city or town; it would have been easier to tell him it was fairyland, because he wished to believe this myth.

---

63 Dick is ill and still working by giving lectures. His money is gone, and he has begun to understand that the final act of his life is about to begin. He decides to tell what he can recall of the studios.

64 Late sixties.

Early Movies

Around the 1900s, film caught on to the imagination of the American public. Theater owners were moving out of the rented stores and lofts where they showed moving pictures reflected on a wall or bedsheet. They discovered they could build theaters in downtown areas, and people would come.

Meanwhile, studio owners turned out two-reelers at a cost of $300 to $3,000 each. As more studios competed to make films, they needed more actors. So they encouraged the stage players to take a fling, and the stars took the dare. However, they tried to do it in secrecy so as to not arouse comment by their friends or managers. They would go over to Fort Lee, New Jersey, and to the various new studios, which were empty warehouses in upper New York. The new industry emphasized a photographic face and a screen personality, because everything was silent with dubbed-in titles. Often, nothing the actor did or pantomimed had any connection with the titles. All the interior shots were actually exterior, as the stages were without roofs to let in the daylight, and if a little rain or snow entered, that too was made a part of the movie. Then, various authorities decided it would be more suitable to film out west in the land of sunshine, and as most filmmakers were in hock to their backers, it was most expedient to leave town and foreclosures behind them.

History of Five Studios

As I said, the studios looked for photographic faces and screen personalities that enticed people into the theaters, which were being developed. The novelty was catching on to the extent that movie theaters were built in downtown areas, and people would go in and see a whole afternoon of film.

To understand the progress from the one- and two-reelers to today's productions and the development of the star system, which led up to the creation of the five major studios in Hollywood—Fox, Paramount, (formerly known as Brunton), Warner Brothers, MGM (Metro-Goldwyn-Mayer), and RKO—we have to go back to the beginning.

Fox Studios

Fox Studios began in 1915 and was down on Western Boulevard, and it was controlled by William Fox and Winfield Sheehan. They made a name for themselves early on when their actress, Janet Gaynor, won the first Academy Award for best actress in *7th Heaven* in 1927 with a fine male lead, Charles Farrell. This picture and *The Iron Horse* (1924) gave Fox Studios great impetus.

They made the first successful comedies, including *A Connecticut Yankee in King Arthur's Court* (1921), which was a great success both financially and publically and gave Fox more importance. After that they came along with *The Iron Horse* (1924), depicting the building of a nation by railroad, which was a tremendous success. As I remember, it opened at the Egyptian Theater in Hollywood, which was one of the first multimillion-dollar deluxe theaters.[65]

They moved up into the big parade bracket with such actors of stature as Theda Bara, Spencer Tracy, John Gilbert, Warner Baxter, George O'Brien, and Ralph Bellamy. They produced *The Big Parade* (1925) and *What Price Glory* (1926), and before this they had been making low-budget pictures with Tom Mix and Buck Jones. They then brought in a man by the name of F.W. Mornau, who made a picture called *Sunrise* (1927) that added to their image, and they rose in importance, as the film incorporated music, which had not been done before.

A young producer, Hal Wallis,[66] one of the great producers of Warner Brothers, was responsible for many of these pictures. Wallis brought in a man by the name of Mervyn LeRoy,[67] a cousin of Jesse Lasky's.[68] LeRoy started out as a gofer and an actor, but he was neither and wound up as a fine director.

In 1933 Darryl Zanuck[69] rose in fame. He began at Warner Brothers, and being an enterprising young man, he left Warner Brothers and formed the 20th Century organization with Joseph M.

---

65 The Egyptian Theater opened in 1922.
66 Best remembered for *Casablanca*. Married actress Martha Hyer (1898–1986).
67 Director and film producer, best known for the *Wizard of Oz* (1900–1987).
68 Pioneer motion-picture producer and key founder with Adolph Zukor of Paramount Pictures.
69 Next to Adolph Zukor, had the longest career in Hollywood. Beginning as a writer, he became a studio head (1902–1979).

Schenck. When Fox began to go down the drain, they stepped in, and by 1935, Fox became 20th Century Fox. Mr. William Fox was no longer head of it, and Winfield Sheehan was relieved of his duties. Zanuck took it over and made it into a great success. Under his keen leadership, it was built into one of the three top organizations in the motion-picture business. For a time Zanuck was relieved of his duties, and it didn't take very long before Fox slumped into a second-rate company. Zanuck came back and rebuilt it again.

Zanuck signed up actors like John Barrymore and Irene Rich. Zanuck made them click, and they became famous. Talking pictures came along in 1925, and they signed up Al Jolson. Actually, Fox made the first talking picture with Jolson, before he went to Warner Brothers for *The Jazz Singer* (1927). By then we knew the handwriting was on the wall, and talkies were here to stay. However, Fox progressed as rapidly as Metro-Goldwyn-Mayer under the guidance of Zanuck.

Paramount

From the early 1900s up to the very peak of its development, this mammoth industry covered a lot of ground. In 1920 the top studio was Famous Players Lasky, or Paramount Pictures, which was the leasing corporation under Adolph Zukor.

The vicar-general of that time at Famous Players Lasky was Cecile B. DeMille[70] (1881–1959), who was brought out here by Jesse Lasky in 1914 to make *The Squaw Man* with Dustin Farnum.

Famous Players was broken up into two parts. Even in those days, there was a minor studio called Real Art, which was a subsidiary of

---

70 Beginning as an actor, he advanced to being a famous film director and producer in both silent and sound.

Paramount and was closer in on Sunset Boulevard, almost down into Los Angeles. At that time they had two stages and two girl stars, Wanda Hawley and Bebe Daniels (1915), who worked exclusively at Real Art because this studio made specialized comedies, which used these girls. They were completely separate and had their own bailiwick at Real Arts Studios. They had their own casting director. It was very intimate. These girls turned out four to six pictures a year.

Paramount then made from fifty-two to fifty-four pictures a year, and each star was scheduled to make so many; if the star's light had gone out, another star who was popular would then have to come in and make up the difference.

Then they began pictures called "specials" later in 1922, such as *The Ten Commandments*, by De Mille, and *The Covered Wagon* (1923), directed by James Cruz. Prior to this time, some effort to make "specials" had begun, such as *The Four Horsemen of the Apocalypse* (1921), directed by Rex Ingram, which brought fame to Valentino; *Broken Blossoms* (1919); and *Intolerance* (1916), both directed by D. W. Griffith.

There were many attempts at elongated pictures, which ran to eight reels. I think *The Ten Commandments* (1956) ran to ten reels and was one of the first pictures, along with *Covered Wagon* (1923), to have an intermission.

Warner Brothers

Warner Brothers[71] Studios began in 1918. It had been a struggling outfit on Sunset Boulevard, under the direction of Jack Warner and his two brothers, Harry and Sam, who were tremendously popular

---

71 Four brothers ran the business empire. Sam and Jack produced, while Harry and Albert controlled and ran the finances.

with everybody. But they built their foundation on Monte Blue, Rin Tin Tin (the dog), and Irene Rich. They lured John Barrymore to the screen, which was a feather in their cap.

They did a talkie with Al Jolson in 1927, and that really put them in business. They moved out into the Valley and built a magnificent plant, one of the most beautiful of all the motion-picture studios, which remains to this day.

The 1940s were the beginning of a whole new era of players, too, because shortly thereafter Warner Brothers created the gangster pictures, which became very popular and created a new genre with stars such as Edward G. Robinson and James Cagney (1930s).

Metro-Goldwyn-Mayer

Metro-Goldwyn-Mayer was not formed until 1924. The old Samuel Goldwyn Studios at Culver City, formed in 1923, were practically out of business and near bankruptcy. They were taken over by Metro Studios, which was then on Cole Avenue in Hollywood in a ramshackle building. The powers that be of Loews' Inc. got together with L. B. Mayer[72] and Al Lickman, sales manager for L. B. Mayer, an independent outfit, and they retained the name of Goldwyn because of its value to the theatrical industry. They formed a new company, took over the old Sam Goldwyn Studios, and renamed it Metro-Goldwyn-Mayer in 1924. The name remains to this day.

Mayer, prior to his time, was out at Selig Zoos with an independent company with Lickman. They were the proud possessors of three stages, as they made animal pictures with such stars as Kathleen Williams, Lewis Stone, and Anita Stewart. They moved

---

72 Famous producer who built MGM and the creator of the "star system" (1884–1957).

the studio from place to place in early motion-picture history, trying to find a more central location. It was almost impossible in the old days to get out to Selig Zoo by any transportation other than automobile, as it was located in East Los Angeles.

Sam Goldwyn[73] had left his partnership with Famous Players Lasky and bought the Triangle Studios in Culver City. He changed the name to Samuel Goldwyn Studios and was not very successful. He had a small group of stars including Will Rogers, Mae Murray, Lew Cody, and a few top-echelon directors. However, the financial structure was too high for Goldwyn to maintain, and the Sam Goldwyn Studios became a defunct organization.

L. B. Mayer, on the other hand, was a very astute showman, and being a progressive person, he built the studio into a position of respected importance in the thirties and forties. Together he and Goldwyn incorporated the stars already under contract to Goldwyn and added a few more to the roster.

That was an early part of motion pictures and shows how they changed by moving from place to place until they found a better place most centrally located to work. As I said, it was almost impossible in the old days to get out to Selig Zoo. When Mayer took over as head of MGM, he inherited whatever stars were left under the Goldwyn banner, namely, Lew Cody and Mae Murry—I think that was about all they had at the time.

Finally, they brought in John Gilbert from Fox and Lon Chaney, who was a great character actor of his day. Mayer made great use of his few stars, and it was the beginning of the building of one of the greatest empires in the motion-picture industry. Soon after this, L.

---

73   Polish American film producer also known as Samuel Goldfish (1879–1974).

B. Mayer began thinking of building a new crop of stars, such as Joan Crawford. He put her in pictures with Owen Moore and Lon Chaney to bring her into prominence.

L. B. Mayer was forthright enough to create more stars in that period than any other producer. Mayer and Goldwyn took John Gilbert away from Fox and made him a tremendous star under Mayer's care. They brought Greta Garbo from Europe and raised her name to the heights of stardom.

By 1934 William Powell, Kay Francis, and Ruth Chatterton did not fare too well under Warner Brothers. It wasn't long before it was almost a swan song for William Powell. In desperation he took a contract with Metro to make a picture in thirteen days. It was called *The Thin Man* (1934), with Myrna Loy, which turned into a tremendous success. Then the series started, and after a few episodes of *The Thin Man*, Powell became one of the top ten male actors in the industry, along with Myrna, a prominent female actress.

They hired Wallace Beery, whom Paramount had dropped, because they thought he couldn't talk. Then Mayer took Louise Dressler out of Mack Sennett comedies, gave her lead roles in pictures such as The Goose Woman (1925), and made a team of Wallace Beery and Marie Dressler in *Min and Bill* (1930), which was probably one of their most important series. They were the only studios that really did a series on a grand scale, such as *The Thin Man*, *Min and Bill*, and *Andy Hardy* (1937), so well that they were not just a run-of-the-mill series of pictures.

By 1929 they were able to compete with the other studios and were running fast enough to catch up with Famous Players Lasky Studios, which had become Paramount Pictures.

RKO

The old RKO Studio never did flourish very well. Then they became Robertson Cole, then RKO (Radio Keith Orpheum), which was next to Paramount on Melrose Avenue after Paramount had moved from Vine Street in 1928. They were really a hit-and-miss organization, a sort of fly-by-night, and they really didn't do anything until David Selznick[74] took over and began to make some pictures with Katharine Hepburn, whom he brought to the screen, Joel McCrea, Constance Bennett, and a few others.

Now RKO began to move forward under the guidance of David Selznick, who had started with Metro-Goldwyn-Mayer, came to Paramount, and left Paramount to take charge of production at the studio on Gower and Melrose.

They then signed a newcomer named Katharine Hepburn, as well as Joel McCrea, whom nobody seemed to pay any attention to until RKO put him under contract and put him opposite Constance Bennett in his first picture, which immediately gave him a name to reckon with. Now they signed up Marion Cooper, a director from the old team of Schoedsack and Cooper, who had made *Chang* (1927) and *Grass* (1925), two big epics[75] in the twenties. Cooper made *King Kong* (1933), which was a tremendous moneymaker. By now they were well established. Richard Dix had left Paramount to sign with RKO and make *Cimarron* (1931) with Irene Dunne. Irene Dunne was an unknown player, a newcomer, but when she played opposite Dix, who had been a recognized star with Paramount for years, her fortune was made.

They brought Fred Astaire and Ginger Rogers and made a great dance team with them (1933–1939). But, as I've said, they've always

---

74 Producer best known for *Gone with the Wind* (1902–1965).
75 Actually documentaries.

been a hit-and-miss organization. To this day nobody knows what makes RKO tick. It no longer exists, because Gulf Western, the company that gobbled up Paramount, purchased Desilu. The old RKO belonged to Desi Arnaz and Lucille Ball, who sold out their interest, and now it is called Paramount West.

About the only great picture that RKO made that I can remember was *Cimarron* (1931), the Academy Award picture with Irene Dunne and Richard Dix. This is the only important picture I can remember outside of Constance Bennett blockbusters and Rogers-Astaire dance pictures.

However, with the change of the star system, Gary Cooper, Charles "Buddy" Rogers, and I came along at Paramount and replaced some of the older and better-known stars such as Richard Dix, Jack Holt, Warner Baxter, and several others. Their salaries as far as Paramount was concerned had gotten out of hand. In actuality they really hadn't; they are nothing compared to today's salaries. At that time Gloria Swanson was making $17,500 a week with a year's contract, Thomas Eighan was making $10,000 a week, and Richard Dix was making $10,000 a week.

Warner Baxter took over the Raoul Walsh role in *Ol' Arizona* as the *Cisco Kid* (1928). However, after he left Paramount, Warner landed on his two feet with 20th Century Fox at a tremendous salary, which brought him back as a star with the Fox Company, prior to their becoming 20th Century Fox. Actually, he kept them on their feet. Another gold mine for 20th Century Fox was Shirley Temple, who came along under the guidance of Zanuck.

With studios now booming and European markets opening daily, competition between the studios grew greater. It was then expedient to put players under contract on long terms with options to trade them to other studios, like so much chattel. Some actors had clauses written into their contracts giving them final say in script choice or billing, choice of leads playing opposite them, and certain protective privileges.

Myron Selznick

Myron Selznick,[76] the son of Lewis J. Selznick, decided to become an actor's agent. I was his sole client. His father's independent studio, Lewis J. Selznick Productions, had been frozen out of business by the major studios and their stars, namely, Owen Moore, Olive Thomas, Elaine Hammerstein, and Lew Cody. These actors had gone to other studios or dropped out of the running, as the actor's life was terribly insecure. Hours were long, and scripts were written during the actual filming while the company waited for the next scene to materialize.

Stuntmen were not used[77] in those days. An actor worth his salt was supposed to risk his neck for his art, and if he injured himself, there was no insurance compensation other than taking up a collection from the people on the lot. More than a few actors relied on the inevitable "passing the hat" sustenance to nurse themselves back to health. There had been a few men who had tried to represent actors, but the studios paid them little heed. The actor had to rely on person-to-person contact. The actor would go to the studios to see the casting director, who had a great deal of power. The casting director, in turn, took the actor to the director who was going to make the picture. There were few producers. They came under the heading of executive-producer,

---

76   Brother of David, which helped him to build his career as the first talent agent (1898–1944).
77   Dick did his own stunts in *Wings*.

such as Hector Turnbull of Brunton Studios, which later became Famous Players.

Around 1930, the battle of the stars assumed great importance. There was a raid on Paramount by Warner Brothers. Myron Selznick, at the time (now one of the most powerful agents in the motion-picture industry), had under contract William Powell, Kay Francis, and Ruth Chatterton. All three were signed up at a combined salary of $30,000 a week on a fifty-two-week contract. He got Constance Bennett $30,000 a week for ten weeks at Warner Brothers, which at this time was absolutely unheard of. This was how difficult it was to get box-office stars. Paramount, however, didn't suffer, as it had many new stars coming along, and their own stars were heavily entrenched as box-office attractions. However, it did cause a lot of bad blood among the different studios.

As I said, when Myron Selznick opened his own agency, I became his client. Actually, I was his sole client until he acquired Kay Francis, Ruth Chatterton, and William Powell. When the day arrived when Paramount Studios failed to acquiesce to Selznick's demands for his clients' welfare, Selznick refused them their services. This caused a furor, an unprecedented challenge, and if military rule had a place in corporate production, the studio heads would have court-martialed their enemy. They likened this hijacking of prices by an actor's agent to the equivalent of a private solder insulting his general. But Selznick stuck to his loaded guns. The tabloids called his interference a "raid." They described his act of interceding for his clients as an act of stealing from the studio, and they condemned the actor for betraying the studio that had nurtured his talents.

As I said, in one fell swoop when Paramount did not accede to Selznick's demands for his clients, he took Kay Francis, Ruth

Chatterton, and William Powell away from Paramount. This was one raid. Kay Francis had made the first picture with Clara Bow and me, *Dangerous Curves*, in 1929. At this time she was a full-fledged star. Ruth Chatterton had been a stage actress, and when talkies came in, she had become a screen star. William Powell, who up to the time of talkies had been a featured player, now became box-office news and a star. Added to these three stars was Constance Bennett, who I mentioned had become the first star to get $30,000 a week on a ten-week guarantee. She was taken. Paramount thought Warner Brothers had lost their minds because she had been paid $300,000 for a ten-week picture, but she was worth ten times her salary in value to the studios as she had tremendous box-office appeal.

As the studios grew in stature, a free-for-all battle of the stars grew in proportion to the status of the studio. Up to this point, the studios did their own hiring and firing of players, writers, directors, and producers. Nobody knew how to represent actors to the studios in script choice or billing, or choice of opposite leads if they were the stars. Now, with agents to intercede, the producers came into their own and could make demands.

In the early days of pictures, there were few actors' agents in the industry. Management and the stars seemed to get along pretty well. I must say in its defense that if you were successful in the motion-picture industry, money was no object. If you became a star, they were the very first ones to tear up your contract and throw it out the window and give you a new one, usually for much more money than you would have asked for.

Mr. Zukor and Mr. Lasky, especially, were very aware of their stars and of their value, and they did everything in the world to make them happy and contented, and publicity-wise they did everything to make them popular. They gave them the best pictures, directors, and stories, so why would you leave and move to another studio?

You stayed until Paramount was sued in a huge antitrust suit by the government in 1948. Then it all ended overnight, and the studio system went down, never to return. I really regretted that. The government said it was not right for the motion-picture companies to own their own theaters and produce pictures at the same time. According to this law, everybody was in violation of the antitrust act. And thanks to the US government, a great industry was destroyed, or at the least, the government was part of its downfall.

It seems to me that with the passing of the star system, a style of showmanship has died; the glow of a once-intangible luminescence cast by the reflection of the magic lantern has slowly been extinguished. The dignity, fun, and color of being a part of this industry no longer exist. Formerly, the show began on the studio lots and ended with a multimillion-dollar epic, premiered by the stars in person. And if fame and fortune followed, who would deny Hollywood's royalty their due, especially when so many hangers-on fluttered on the periphery of the light?

The glamour associated with picture making zoomed the industry. I can't imagine any other business that could possibly be built on the reverberations of a Polish bombshell named Pola Negri, the sultriness of a Theda Bara; the pantomimic skills of a Charles Chaplin, or the sophistication of a Gloria Swanson. It was the day of the artist building an empire and the empire protecting its builders. The Golden Era in film town made the fabled goose that laid the golden egg a brash counterfeit.

Now, that is the saga of the old west in brief, as far as the history of the major studios in Hollywood.

Perhaps one day I will bump into the gas-station attendant in St. Louis. More likely, we will meet on Hollywood and Vine. If he and his missus finally arrived in film town and haven't yet been disillusioned by the factories that turn out our product, I will be surprised. He may be younger in spirit than I thought him and found his bag on Sunset Strip with the hippies.

Recollections of Early Hollywood—1975

I DECIDED TO TAKE ONE last nostalgic walk down where the town of Hollywood used to be with Maxine. Hollywood used to end at the corner of the First National Bank Building (corner of Highland Avenue and Hollywood Boulevard). Across the street was the old Bank of America, which we used in so many pictures in the early twenties and thirties. Then there were the old Hollywood Theater and the Montmartre Café, which were left of the bank. As I walked down the street, I noticed the brass stars in the sidewalk. Here were Ingrid Bergman, Buster Keaton, Paul Whiteman, Bing Crosby, and my own star. As I walked and kept passing the stars in the cement, I couldn't help thinking of how many had passed away.

I recalled the lovely cafés where you sat outside, the palm trees, and the red cars going back and forth. For some reason or other, and it wasn't nostalgic, I was looking at Hollywood Boulevard not as it is today, but as I first knew it forty-nine years ago, (1920's) with its sidewalk cafés sheltered by gay umbrellas and palm trees (now replaced by red maples), the red cars going back and forth, when you could travel from Los Angeles to Hollywood for five cents, believe it or not.

The Red Cars (1870–1961)

There used to be streetcar tracks that ran down the middle of Hollywood Boulevard. In the old days, the streetcars cost five cents and were very popular and lent a particular flavor to Hollywood. Some of the cars were outdoor cars, as California was noted for its warm climate. Some of the red cars had benches that faced the sidewalk, and you could sit side by side to watch the people walking up and down. Sometimes we would walk down the boulevard at night. If we were tired, we would stop, get on the cars, and say "hello" to everyone. The cars ran every ten or twelve minutes. You would put your nickel in for the conductor and sit down. There were steps along the side of the streetcar, and you could get off wherever you wanted to get off, as they would pause. They didn't go fast, because people were on the boulevard, and there was a great deal of traffic. The tourists wanted to go slowly and see Hollywood Boulevard.

The cars went from Los Angeles to the end of Hollywood. One red car ran from the station on Third and Hill Street through the Hill Street tunnel out Sunset Boulevard and finally divided at 4500 Sunset Boulevard, where Hollywood divides. Hollywood continues, and Sunset, which is in the shape of a V, continued on out, but there were no streetcars on that street. The car traveled on Hollywood Boulevard, and when it got down to La Brea, it went down a freeway, and the ride ended at Gardner Junction. They called it Gardner Junction because sometimes you had to get off of that car and take another car to Santa Monica. The otwher car ran down Santa Monica Boulevard and out all the way to the beach at Santa Monica. The third red car ran from Washington Boulevard, in downtown Los Angeles, out to Venice by way of Culver City, which is where MGM Studios stands today. The Hal Roach studios are gone. Those were the famous comedy studios, which had Bebe Daniels and Harold Lloyd.

On the other side of the street, there was once the Carlton Café. Where there once had been orange groves was now the Hollywood Egyptian Theater. Up one way was the Hollywood Movie, where we went for ten cents, and down the other way was the Iris Theater, which cost ten cents also. Now the street was full of different shops, and it was hard to recall that at one time the street was full of theaters. This went on up until the thirties and forties, but now all is forgotten.

The so-called wild parties were held on Thursday nights in the old Hollywood Hotel, which was on Vine Street and Hollywood Boulevard. The hotel took in about four or five or more acres. It was a lovely, old, rambling hotel about three stories high with its awnings and wide verandas. That hotel was the beginning of the residential area of Hollywood Boulevard. Next to it was Garden Court Apartments, and then farther out on Hollywood were the homes of Joseph Schenck, Betty Compson, Norma Tallmadge, and many stars of that era, as well as the four-acre estate of Jack Holt.

In the middle of Hollywood was the Christy Hotel and smaller hotels of some twenty or thirty rooms. From 1920 to 1928, new hotels were built, like the Roosevelt Hotel on Hollywood Boulevard and, as I said, the new Christy Hotel. It was evident the old Hollywood Hotel was in a state of decay. It was such a shame taking down this old hotel, because it was a landmark.

Up from Hollywood Boulevard were the Whitley Heights, a very fashionable area between Highland Avenue and Cahuenga. It was a beautiful section, and some of the stars such as Rudolph Valentino and Barbara LaMarr lived there. Franklin Avenue became desirable; it was an extension that led toward the Hollywood Bowl and then traveled out into the San Fernando Valley. But Hollywood was the place. All the stars lived in Hollywood, as Beverly Hills was unknown at that time.

The smart address for bachelors in the motion-picture industry was the Hollywood Athletic Club where I lived. There were cute bungalows and courts just off Hollywood Boulevard down McCadden and Las Palmas.

The downtown part of Hollywood extended from Highland and Gower Street, where the Christy Studios and the Columbia and Sunshine Comedies were. From Vine Street onward started Hollywood proper, the real Hollywood, with the cute little restaurants, Henri's and the Brass Rail. Almost every night people gathered at these two places to meet and share dinner. At noon, the sidewalk cafes like Armstrong's and Musso & Frank's (still in existence) were filled. Musso & Frank's befriended many an actor and fed him when he was down and out, never questioning the bill. The amazing thing was that actors rarely failed to pay Musso & Frank's back because the owner was always so good to them. It was like a small town, and we knew every shopkeeper along the way and knew we were home on those streets.

The Old Montmartre Café (1920s) on Highland was entered on the second floor. Eddie Branstetter owned it, and at night it was the place to go for all the young Joan Crawfords and starlets of that era. They were busy chewing up the floor to the tune of "The Charleston" while Red Nichols or some wonderful orchestra of the day played all night. You could have a terrific evening for ten dollars.

Baseball and the Beach

Monday through Saturday was busy, but Sunday was special in Hollywood. Baseball was in its heyday, and on the corner of Hollywood and Cahuenga was a big, vacant square. The fire department was about 150 yards below Hollywood Boulevard, and they prided themselves on having a very fine baseball team.

Every Sunday morning Buster Keaton and some of the stars of that day would gather and play the fire department. By noon, the place was lined with admirers up and down Hollywood and Cahuenga. Most of the time, the fire department won; it didn't matter who was batting. Now and then they were kind and would let us win.

The moment the game was over, we would rush to our cars and head for Santa Monica and Crystal Pier, which was the gathering place way before beach clubs. We'd go to the pier with its great amusement park. To the right was Crystal Beach, and we called it

Crystal Pier. At one time there were studios all along the pier. The Nat Goodwin studios were there. Almost every day some comedy company would be making a picture on that pier.

In the early twenties, we went out to the beach. We went out on Santa Monica Boulevard, which was a funny little road like a bent ribbon, just wide enough for two cars. We would go through all these bean fields and flower fields.

At that time Venice was supposed to be a replica of Venice, Italy. There were hundreds of canals that intertwined and interlocked and went to the sea. The canals are still in existence, but the attempt to recreate Venice ended.

Before there were beach clubs, there was Crystal Pier. There was a sailing fraternity. Very few of the stars were boat minded in those days, with the exception of John Barrymore (who came later). Boating did not become fashionable until 1922 or 1923 with Thomas H. Ince and Randolph Hearst with his boats. Zane Grey, the author, owned one of the most magnificent boats I have ever seen, *The Fisherman*, which was a 250-foot schooner.

NIGHTCLUBS

There was a famous nightclub at the top of the hill (and this was Prohibition) called the Sunset Inn. Farther down at Venice, in the shape of a ship built out over the water, with an interior that was exactly the same as a ship at sea, was the Ships Café. When nighttime came and we were all through at the beach, those that had enough money would go to either the Sunset Inn in Santa Monica or the Ships Café in Venice for dinner and would drink Hollywood gin, neatly bottled in bottles that resembled Gordon's Gin, labels and all. However, it was really bathtub gin.

Beverly Hills

Beverly Hills at that time did not amount to anything as a residential section. In fact, Beverly Hills was not even heard of, except for a speedway. There weren't any hotels other than the old Beverly Hills Hotel, which was surrounded by vegetable farms, primarily lettuce farms. Beverly Hills really began in 1924 or 1925 when they started to subdivide. The perfection of that city can be attributed to four or five people...including Will Rogers, Harold Lloyd, Conrad Nagel, Mary Pickford, and Doug Fairbanks. They were the ones who helped lay it out. It was decided that the mayor of Beverly Hills would earn a yearly salary of one dollar (still in effect to this day).

On the corner of Wilshire Boulevard and La Brea, there was a flying field, which belonged to Cecil B. DeMille, and there was also Clover Field at Santa Monica. Aviation was very young.

Early Days of Movies

I'll go back to the early days, the 1920s, when Hollywood mostly comprised several major studios: the William Fox Studios; Paramount Studios, which was then Famous Players; Universal Studios; Metro; Sam Goldwyn Studios, who were semimajor; and Brunton. There were twenty or thirty independent studios. There also was the Hal Roach Studios, which was strictly comedy.

The industry, young as it was, was strictly under the control of its founders. These were men who knew the basics of the business. Therefore, it was a well-managed industry. Paramount finally took over Brunton. It was a very tightly knit group, and regardless of who was in charge, the heads always remained the same, such as Zukor and Lasky, until the stock-market crash of 1929. When I first went to Famous Players, the head was Hector Turnbull; later it was Schulberg, and after that Manny Cohen. There was tremendous loyalty among the directors and producers; there were 3,500 employees, and it was "one for all and all for one." This also took place at MGM after they amalgamated with Louie Mayer and took over the Goldwyn Studios. Mayer ruled with an iron hand and built his group of actors into one of great magnitude. He started with a small nucleus of players such as John Gilbert (who came over from Fox Studios, where he was a big star), and he developed Joan Crawford. When he took over the studio, all he had was Mae Murray, Lon

Chaney, and Louis Stone. And from that group, he built MGM into one of the largest and most illustrious of all studios.

Paramount, on the other hand, went along on an even keel. They were the Bank of America type of institution. They did not have any problem with players. We used to advertise "More stars than there are in heaven," and this was true. They had a great faculty for picking people. They began to pick new people such as Gary Cooper, Buddy Rogers, and me. They have always had a very strong roster of stars, such as James Hall, Thomas Meehan, Richard Dix, Gloria Swanson, Bebe Daniels, Esther Ralston, and Wallace Beery, who was not really a star in his own name. They developed the team of Beery and Hatton that did nothing but make tremendous amounts of money (they made almost five hundred movies). They had William S. Hart, Jack Holt, and Florence Vidor. These were stars of the early twenties that many people won't recollect. From this group the new players were given a chance to come in. The new players were matched up with the older actors in lesser roles in order to learn their trade. When Shemberg came in, he brought Clara Bow with him. She was a tremendous asset. The loyalty of the studios was amazing. Fox was very close with Janet Gaynor, Charlie Farrell, Tom Mix, and Buck Jones.

The studios in the beginning years emphasized westerns. They quickly became the backbone of the industry. People love the charm and character of the West. I have always believed in the strength of the western fable. It was only fitting that Hollywood would make the first adult western and begin a new passage into the Wild West of movies with features such as *The Virginian*.

As Maxine and I walked along, my memories came flooding back with all the good fortune I had known. It was truly the golden age of motion pictures. I had been a part of that beginning, that time, and had personally witnessed the evolution of film. I was fortunate enough to have experienced the greatness of *Wings* and been a part of the first Academy Awards. I held on tight to Max's hand, and we moved on down the boulevard.

Epilogue

~

Alice asked the Cheshire Cat, who was sitting in a tree, "What road do I take?"
The cat asked, "Where do you want to go?"
"I don't know", Alice answered.
"Then", said the cat, "it really doesn't matter does it?"
>---Lewis Carroll, "Alice's Adventures in Wonderland" starring Richard Arlen as the Cheshire Cat (released in 1933).

ONE EVENING, SEVERAL YEARS AGO, a friend and I went to the L.B. Mayer theater at the Motion Picture Home. We had come to see a famous actor debut his one act autobiographical play. Now in his 90's, recovering from a stroke, he appeared frail as he entered the darkened stage.

This was a man who had had tremendous success, both in writing books and acting in films. Following in his footsteps, his son was now a famous actor himself. His life was rich and fulfilled. He smiled, greeted us and began to tell his tale.

His life was a story of cruel and impoverished beginnings. An immigrant's son, he had left home at age 16. He never dreamt he would find his way in acting nor accomplish and receive as many honors as he had received. Now, near the end of his life, he found himself surrounded by family with riches far beyond the dreams of a poor Jewish boy from the tenements.

We listened and applauded. Then, at a sudden and inexplicable point he began to talk about his father, a cruel, brutal, abusive alcoholic. This was the man he had run away from. He was the impetus for his need to escape, to be noticed, to find a meaning to his life, to be "a star".

At the end of his life his father had asked for him. Could he say goodbye? Was it possible to forgive this man he had not seen in years? Haunted by his past, he refused and left his father to die alone.

He turned to the audience and spoke with his hands twisting in the air. "All I ever wanted" he said in a wavering voice, "was to hear my father say he loved me". He looked down at the floor and sadly half whispered, "and he never did". I was struck by the need of this man to have one simple thing given to him…the love and acceptance of his father. And realized he was looking back with deep regrets, sorrow and pain. I thought of Dick whose early life had been such a contrast to his.

Each of us is born with great promise and hope. Every journey is different. Some are blessed with good fortune and luck in their beginnings. Sometimes there is only hardship. All good things come if we work hard enough…isn't that the end of the fairy tale? And all live happily ever after. But what if dreams fall apart?

Richard's life, so full of success early on, had taken a different turn. His third marriage had not worked out. They quietly separated. After fifty years of hard work he found himself broke, alone, and forgotten.

Dearest
So you can keep
a record of the
family. Love of Md,
Deri

Then he met Maxine. My mother loved him for all the things he had been. Nobody could laugh at his jokes as she did or listen and write the stories that now he was consumed with telling.

She worked on the book for six years after he died, unable to publish it. All she had were the tapes of his wonderful voice talking to her and telling her his memories.

What I first found in 2008 were endless pages going nowhere. Spreading the yellowed, hand typed papers from wall to wall, reading them carefully, the book slowly began to take shape. Choosing his biography and the many stories, and in particular, WINGS, was a decision that was difficult to make. His biography was wonderful. As he stated, he had led a Tom Sawyer life. The stories were equally good. Dick said in the opening passages, "he needed to tell it like it was". Reflecting on Hollywood after half a century of being a working actor was the summation of his life.

Richard's fables took us through that door with him. His recollections showed that there is a wondrous point, no matter the ending, to the dance of life. Through his voice we heard the music, became the dancer, and moved effortlessly through those moments with him.

What are we if we are not our "memories"?

He loved her. She loved him. Together they shared a moment in time. Dick's voice was strong. Mom's was equal to his. They lived on in the only gift he could leave to her --- himself. Goodnight, sweet dreams and know that the story was finally told.

Richard's 250the movie—name unknown—sometime in 1958

Filmography

MOVIE	YEAR
A whale of a Tale	1977
Won Ton Ton: The Dog who Saved Hollywood	1976
Walt Disney's Wonderful World of Color (TV Series)	1975
The Sky's the Limit	1975
Cade's County (TV Series)	1971
Rogues Gallery	1968
Anzio	1968
Buckskin	1968
The Road to Nashville	1967
The Lucy Show (TV Series)	1967
Fort Utah	1967
Hostile Guns	1967
Red Tomahawk	1967
Waco	1966
To the Shores of Hell	1966
Johnny Reno	1966
Apache Uprising	1965
The Bounty Killer	1965
Town Tamer	1965
Black Spurs	1965
Branded (TV Series)	1965
The Human Duplicators	1965

Young Fury	1965
Sex and the College Girl	1964
The Shepherd of the Hills	1964
The Best Man	1964
Law of the Lawless	1964
The Crawling Hand	1963
The New Breed (TV Series)	1962
The Last Time I Saw Archie	1961
Perry Mason (TV Series)	1961
Lawman (TV Series)	1959-1961
Michael Shayne (TV Series)	1961
Lock Up (TV Series)	1961
Bat Masterson (TV Series)	1959-1961
Ripcord (TV Series)	1961
The Best of the Post (TV Series)	1960
Coronado 9 (TV Series)	1960
Raymie	1960
Whirlybirds (TV Series)	1960
Yancy Derringer (TV Series)	1959
Wagon Train (TV Series)	1959
Warlock	1959
Wanted: Dead or Alive (TV Series)	1959
Cavalry Command	1958
Crossroads (TV Series)	1956-1957
Playhouse 90 (TV Series)	1957
The 20th Century-Fox Hour (TV Series)	1957
The Mountain	1956
Climax (TV Series)	1956
Matinee Theatre (TV Series)	1955-1956
Hidden Guns	1956
TV Reader's Digest	1956
Blonde Blackmailer	1955
The Whistler (TV Series)	1955

Science Fiction Theatre (TV Series)	1955
The Loretta Young Show (TV Series)	1955
Devil's Harbor	1954
Alarm (TV Movie)	1954
Sabre Jet	1953
The Blazing Forest	1952
Hurricane Smith	1952
Flaming Feather	1952
Silver City	1951
Nash Airflyte Theatre (TV Series)	1951
Kansas Raiders	1950
Grand Canyon	1949
When My Baby Smiles at Me	1948
The Return of Wildfire	1948
Speed to Spare	1948
Buffalo Bill Rides Again	1947
Accomplice	1946
The Phantom Speaks	1945
Identity Unknown	1945
The Big Bonanza	1944
Storm Over Lisbon	1944
That's My Baby!	1944
The Lady and the Monster	1944
Timber Queen	1944
Minesweeper	1943
Submarine Alert	1943
Alaska Highway	1943
Aerial Gunner	1943
Wrecking Crew	1942
A Letter from Bataan (Short)	1942
Wildcat	1942
Torpedo Boat	1942
Flying Blind	1941

A Dangerous Game	1941
Raiders of the Desert	1941
Forced Landing	1941
Power Dive	1941
Men of the Timberland	1941
Mutiny in the Arctic	1941
Lucky Devils	1941
The Devil's Pipeline	1940
The Leather Pushers	1940
Black Diamonds	1940
Hot Steel	1940
Danger on Wheels	1940
The Man from Montreal	1939
Legion of Lost Flyers	1939
Tropic Fury	1939
Mutiny on the Blackhawk	1939
Missing Daughters	1939
Straight Place and Show	1938
Call of the Yukon	1938
No Time to Marry	1938
Murder in Greenwich Village	1937
Artists and Models	1937
Silent Barriers	1937
Secret Valley	1937
The Mine with the Iron Door	1936
Three Live Ghosts	1936
The Calling of Dan Matthews	1935
Let 'em Have It	1935
Helldorado	1935
Ready for Love	1934
She Made Her Bed	1934
Come On, Marines!	1934
Alice in Wonderland	1933

Hell and High Water	1933
Golden Harvest	1933
Three Cornered Moon	1933
College Humor	1933
Song of the Eagle	1933
Island of Lost Souls	1932
The All-American	1932
Tiger Shark	1932
Guilty as Hell	1932
Sky Bride	1932
Wayward	1932
Touchdown	1931
Caught	1931
The Secret Call	1931
The Lawyer's Secret	1931
Gun Smoke	1931
The Conquering Horde	1931
Only Saps Work	1930
The Santa Fe Trail	1930
The Sea God	1930
Galas de la Paramount	1930
The Border Legion	1930
Paramount on Parade	1930
The Light of Western Stars	1930
Dangerous Paradise	1930
Burning Up	1930
The Virginian	1929
Dangerous Curves	1929
Thunderbolt	1929
The Four Feathers	1929
The Man I Love	1929
Manhattan Cocktail	1928
Beggars of Life	1928

Ladies of the Mob	1928
Feel My Pulse	1928
Under the Tonto Rim	1928
She's a Sheik	1927
Figures Don't Lie	1927
Sally in Our Alley	1927
The Blood Ship	1927
Rolled Stockings	1927
Wings	1927
Old Ironsides	1926
You'd Be Surprised	1926
Padlocked	1926
Behind the Front	1926
The Enchanted Hill	1926
The Coast of Folly	1925
In the Name of Love	1925
Sally	1925
The Fighting Coward	1924
Vengeance of the Deep	1923
Quicksands	1923
The Ghost Breaker	1922
The Green Temptation	1922
Ladies Must Live	1921

RICHARD PLAYING HIMSELF (23 Credits)

It was a Very Good Year (TV Series)	1971
Johnny Carson Presents the Sun City Scandals '70 (TV Movie)	1970
Petticoat Junction (TV Series)	1968
Here's Hollywood (TV Series)	1961
This is Your Life (TV Series)	1955-1961
About Faces (T Series)	1960
The Colgate Comedy Hour (TV Series)	1955
Your Show of Shows (TV Series)	1951

Filmography

Texaco Star Theatre (TV Series)	1951
The Ed Wynn Show (TV Series)	1950
Unusual Occupations (Documentary Short)	1942
Soaring Stars (Short)	1942
Screen Snapshots Series 19, No. 9: Sports in Hollywood (Documentary Short)	1940
Swing with Bing (Short)	1940
Screen Snapshots Series 15, No. 3 (Documentary short)	1935
Hollywood Hobbies (Documentary Short)	1935
Hollywood on Parade No. B-6 (Short)	1934
How to Break 90 #4: Downswing (Short)	1933
Hollywood on Parade No. A-9 (Short)	1933
Hollywood on Parade No. A-6 (Short)	1933
The Voice of Hollywood No. 12 (Short)	1930
A Trip Through the Paramount Studio (short)	1927
Hollywood	1923

About the Author

Born in Chicago, Judy Watson has always lived in the realm of creativity and the arts. She studied writing at Arizona State University, and she has written short stories and presented a small narrative history. Her brother was an illustrator in film and TV, and her husband was an award-winning TV cameraman. Her son is presently a writer and executive producer at DreamWorks, while her daughter is a gifted artist and photographer who worked for years in animation.

When her mother left hidden photographs, books, letters, manuscripts, tapes, and diaries to Watson, she knew she needed to make this compelling firsthand look inside the golden age of Hollywood available to the public.

She has three grandchildren and currently lives with her two dogs and three cats in Westlake Village, California, where she has been for the past forty-seven years. *"Wings" and Other Recollections of Early Hollywood* is her first book.

Made in the USA
San Bernardino, CA
12 January 2016